DIS MEM BER

Center Point
Large Print

Also by Joyce Carol Oates and available from Center Point Large Print:

Jack of Spades
The Doll-Master

DIS MEM BER

and Other Stories of Mystery and Suspense

Joyce Carol Oates

CENTER POINT LARGE PRINT
THORNDIKE, MAINE

This Center Point Large Print edition is published
in the year 2017 by arrangement with
The Mysterious Press, an imprint of Grove Atlantic.

The text of this Large Print edition is unabridged.
In other aspects, this book may vary
from the original edition.
Printed in the United States of America
on permanent paper.
Set in 16-point Times New Roman type.

ISBN: 978-1-68324-431-8

Library of Congress Cataloging-in-Publication Data

Names: Oates, Joyce Carol, 1938– author.
Title: Dis mem ber : and other stories of mystery and suspense / Joyce
Carol Oates.
Description: Center Point Large Print edition. | Thorndike, Maine :
Center Point Large Print, 2017.
Identifiers: LCCN 2017014433 | ISBN 9781683244318
       (hardcover : alk. paper)
Subjects: LCSH: Large type books. | BISAC: FICTION / Thrillers. |
FICTION / Short Stories (single author). | FICTION / Suspense. |
GSAFD: Mystery fiction. | Suspense fiction.
Classification: LCC PS3565.A8 A6 2017b | DDC 813/.54—dc23
LC record available at https://lccn.loc.gov/2017014433

to Henri Cole

Contents

DIS MEM BER
1.

Tell us what you know. What you remember.

I have climbed up onto the roof of my grandfather's old barn. The tin is hot against my bare legs, thighs. This is a forbidden place. The slanted roof, the ill-fitted rusted sheets of tin scalding-hot in the sun.

I am not so young any longer, to be climbing up on the barn roof. We stopped climbing on the roof by eighth grade.

You forget. You lose interest. Other things to do.

Things you did as a child, even forbidden things you disdain when you are a few years older.

He's driving his Chevy along Iron Road. Bright sky-blue with chrome fixtures that gleam like winking eyes. Inside, cream-colored upholstery. Stains on the back seat he'd tried to wipe off with something strong-smelling like kerosene so all four windows have to be kept open to air out the bad smell.

He's smoking a cigarette. Smoke wreathes his narrow handsome face like a doll's face. Left forearm dangling out the rolled-down window. Ahead is the two-lane blacktop road shimmering in the heat like a desert mirage.

Along Iron Road to Mill Pond Road that is mostly gravel and dirt. Pastures, cornfields, woods. Farmhouses, farm buildings. Silos. The sky-blue Chevy slows, the driver is frowning through dark-tinted aviator glasses like a hunter in no hurry, taking his time.

It is said that Rowan Billiet is my mother's (step)-cousin.

It is said (by my father) that as far as he's concerned Rowan Billiet is no relation to any of us, at all.

It is certainly not true that Rowan Billiet is my *uncle.* He is not the younger brother of either my father or my mother and so he can't be my *uncle.* But like other inaccuracies published in local newspapers this would be repeated and pass into general (mis)understanding and decades later recalled in the vague way we recall terrible dreams that have faded into memories like faded water-stains in wallpaper.

That young uncle of yours, what was his name . . .

The good-looking one always drove fancy cars . . .

Turns onto the Cattaraugus Creek Road which is our road. Is Rowan Billiet idly cruising in the hilly countryside north of Strykersville, has he no particular destination? Seeing where the sky-blue Chevy takes him?

Like dowsing for water. That kind of chance.

Rowan has relatives scattered through Beechum County. Not one of them a close relative, not one what you'd call *family*.

Rowan turns up at their homes, just to say *hello*. Sometimes Rowan stays only a few minutes, sensing that this isn't a good time, or maybe the person he has come to see isn't home. Sometimes Rowan stays longer for instance for supper if he's invited.

Rowan is never invited to stay for supper at our house. The reason seems to be (I have gathered) that my father hates him.

Why'd anybody hate Rowan Billiet!—in the Chevy smelling of kerosene and cigarette smoke he's smiling to himself at such a notion. Humming with music on the car radio turned up high to hear above the wind rushing through opened windows. Tap-tap-tapping his slender fingers on the steering wheel.

Fingers like a girl's fingers, it is said of Rowan Billiet.

Face like a doll's face, it is said of Rowan Billiet.

Why you could not take him seriously even his name: Rowan Billiet.

The year between seventh and eighth grades was like many years and not just a single year.

Growing up we'd played in the junked cars, trucks, tractors in the lot beside my uncle's house.

11

My father's older (half) brother Mason who owned a gas station and auto repair on the Cattaraugus Creek Road a mile from our house.

Our farmhouse where we lived with my mother's (step)-parents who were (a fact I would not learn for decades) not strangers to my mother's biological parents but the brother and sister-in-law of her parents.

All that had happened long ago, before I was born. I had not the slightest awareness nor would I have the slightest interest for many years until I was at least the age of my mother at the time Rowan Billiet came into my life in a special way in 1961.

My uncle's sprawling junkyard was a forbidden place too. We were not wanted there. Easy to injure yourself. If you were a girl it was especially easy, we were warned.

Our bare knees scratched, bleeding. Rivulets of blood on my legs from where glass slivers had cut me as I'd squeezed through the broken window of a car "totaled" in a wreck about which people still spoke in hushed whispers along the Cattaraugus Creek Road. Thrilled because I was the smallest of the five of us who hung out together (three girls, two boys who were our younger brothers) and the only one able to squeeze through so narrow and twisted a space and later when my mother saw me she'd stared for a moment before realizing these were just shallow scratches on my legs and the bright blood could be wiped easily away.

Oh God! You scared me, Jill. . . .

In my uncle's junkyard there was an old hulk of a tow truck with a giant hook covered in rust like blood. It was frightening to see this hook and to imagine such a large hook somehow—*hooked*—into living flesh. . . .

Tell us what you recall, Jill.

Anything you recall.

Take your time. Try not to be upset. It is all over now, you are not in any danger.

He's saying there's something he wants to show me.

He's calling me *Jill-y*. His special way of saying my name which is not the way other people say it.

Look, *Jill-y*. Just a little drive to the bridge and back.

Rowan Billiet would always stand a little too close. Smiling with his lower lip caught in his teeth.

I can't, I guess. Not right now.

Why not, *not right now? Right now* is the best fuckin time.

This makes me giggle. Nobody talks to girls my age the way Rowan Billiet does when there are no adults to hear.

Giggling like I am being tickled with hard fast fingers. It is unsettling and exciting and makes my heart quicken but not in a happy way.

Rowan Billiet is not a high school boy but he is not old like my father and uncles. You'd have a hard time describing him. He makes you laugh. He makes you laugh *funny*—like you don't know why you are laughing, and would not want an adult to overhear and to ask why you are laughing, what's *so funny*.

My friends who've seen Rowan Billiet say he looks like a lighter-haired and shorter Elvis Presley. He is very good-looking with sand-colored hair fine like the silk of milkweed that falls in a wave over his forehead, sand-colored eyebrows and a little mustache like a sand-colored caterpillar on his upper lip.

This little caterpillar-mustache moves on his lip when he talks and when he smiles. Seeing it makes me shiver.

I don't know how to reply to Rowan Billiet when he says these words and so he says again, slow and patient: It's something in the creek, beneath the bridge. It's something that got stuck in the rocks there, from upstream. You'll get a kick out of it, *Jill-y*.

Get a kick out of it. This is a strange thing I have heard people say, that is baffling to me but makes me smile.

And Rowan smiles harder, pulling at my wrist.

14

Rowan can circle my wrist with just his first finger and his thumb.

What you're gonna see, Jill-y, it's just between you and me. You tell anybody else and they ain't gonna understand.

I'm shaking my head saying I guess not.

Yeh c'mon. Nobody will know.

My mother will know. . . .

How the fuck's Irene gonna know if you don't tell her? Looks like nobody's home here anyway.

The way Rowan says *Irene* makes me know that Rowan Billiet knows my mother as I can't know her and there is something familiar and sneering about Rowan's knowledge of her.

I don't want to tell Rowan *Mommy is just out shopping in Ransomville, she will be back any minute.* I don't want Rowan to know that no adult is in our house right now except my grandmother who spends all her time between the kitchen and her (downstairs, blind-drawn) bedroom and would not notice the sky-blue Chevy pulled just halfway into the cinder drive. If she saw Rowan Billiet she would think he's one of my brother's friends from high school anyway.

Afterward I would think—*He knew to come when Mommy was gone. When Daddy wasn't here.*

It is rare for my mother to be gone from the house at any hour of a weekday but it is usual for my father to be gone working at the GM radiator factory in Strykersville.

15

Rowan is frowning like he is trying very hard to remain patient. Giving me another chance.

It's a secret, see? Jill-y?

You tell anybody else and they ain't gonna understand.

You tell anybody else and you'll never get taken for a ride in my Chevy again.

It has not happened that I have ever had a ride in Rowan Billiet's Chevy so (possibly) Rowan is mistaking me for another young-girl cousin.

You coming? O.K.?

I don't say *yes*. But I don't say *no*.

A fever rushes into my face when Rowan pokes my wrist with his forefinger.

All that will happen has not begun yet. Rowan Billiet lifts his aviator sunglasses so that his small shiny-glass eyes move on me winking in the sun.

C'mon, Jill-y. Climb in.

Lemme shut that fuckin door so's it catches.

Tell us what you remember. When did it start.

. . . was there a time when you began to think, this is not right. There is something wrong.

Or did you not ever think that? Were you too young, too intimidated by him? Which?

Riding in the sky-blue Chevy is exciting to me.

From the start Rowan favors *me*.

Later it will be revealed that the sky-blue Chevy was given to Rowan by a friend (from Port

16

Oriskany) or possibly it had been sold to Rowan for so low a price it was practically a gift. Also the expensive-looking wristwatch Rowan wore on his left wrist that fitted him loosely even with the strap adjusted so you could figure it had belonged to a much larger man.

My father would say why in hell would anybody give Rowan Billiet anything, for Christ's sake. The thought seemed to infuriate him as it did other men like my father who worked for every-thing they owned and were rarely given presents of much more consequence than neckties, socks, belts and subtly misshapen hand-knitted sweaters from female relatives.

Once when my father spoke disgustedly of Rowan Billiet my mother told him not to be mean-spirited, that *poor Rowan* had a hard time without any family to speak of.

You should feel sorry for Rowan, not hateful.

My mother felt some kind of guilt for Rowan Billiet. That her family hadn't done much for him when he'd been a small boy and (this was vague to me like all things that had happened before I was born) his parents had broken up and lived in separate places and when Rowan was just a baby he was shuttled between them or maybe not-much-wanted by either and then his mother died, maybe hadn't died but been killed, strangled by some man she'd gotten involved with and so Rowan had been brought to live for a while with my mother's elderly grandparents but after a few years that ended too.

He'd dropped out of school at sixteen. He'd gotten in trouble, or had flunked all his grades, or had just quit because he hated school and hated being told what to do. This was not so unusual, many farm boys did not finish school but Rowan Billiet wasn't a farm boy, he had no farm family and he would inherit no property in Beechum County.

It was said of Rowan Billiet that he'd learned to *make his own way* and this was said with a kind of grudging approval but always as if there was something more to say that wasn't going to be said if there were children within earshot.

My father did not always lower his voice even when children were present. When he was annoyed, or contemptuous. Saying now to my mother, Christ! That little faggot. Don't let me catch him coming around here.

And my mother protested: That's ridiculous! That's really nasty. Why are you saying such a thing, it isn't even true. . . .

On his way out of the house my father laughed harshly as if my mother had said something very stupid that did not deserve a reply.

Faggot. We did not (yet) know what *faggot* meant but we understood that it was an ugly word that girls would not ever use. Nor did it seem like a word our mothers might use.

Instead it was a word used exclusively by men and older boys intent upon expressing contempt, disgust, reproach and a kind of incredulous bemusement and what was special about *faggot* was that it was directed (we observed wonderingly) only toward another male.

Yeh. You're gonna get a kick out of this.

At the bridge Rowan Billiet takes hold of my wrist to lead me down the steep path to the creek. His forefinger and thumb gripping my wrist hard enough to leave a red mark.

It is just a playful gesture, I am thinking. The way my grandfather runs his callused fingers through my hair and I am not supposed to flinch or whimper or cry for that will hurt Grandpa's feelings.

Beneath the bridge there is a large dark rectangular shadow in the water that is the shadow of the bridge rippling like something alive and breathing. The shallow water near shore is heaped with rocks but also concrete rubble and rusted iron rods and it is here that Rowan pulls me toward to see something that looks at first like slow-bobbing clothes or rags or something woolly. Unless I shut my eyes (as Rowan would not allow me to do) there is nowhere else to look.

See? That's something ain't it, lookit the size of that.

Rowan makes a thin whistling sound. I don't

understand what I am seeing. My eyes blink and swell with moisture. And the strong smell of it, that comes up in hot wafts like heat from a vent in the floor, that makes me feel faint.

Rowan is saying he figures it got dumped upstream. There is an excitement in Rowan's voice I have not heard before.

And floated down here and got caught in the rocks. Really something ain't it?

D'you know what "eks-sang-u-ated" is? Blood all gone.

That's what happened here. Like a pig upside down, or a chicken. *Bled out.*

See how it's in parts? See, I can push them. The head is loose from the body. . . . I did that.

Just for the hell of it, fuckin around with my stained-steel Jap knife.

Christ sake! Nobody's gonna hurt *you.*

It's a fancy knife. Cost twelve dollars. Stained-steel made in Japan.

Want to hold it? No?

Like this, sawed through the "vert-e-bray."

Know what "vert-e-bray" is, Jill-y? Like, your spine.

Here's your spine, see? Up here too. Your neck is like your spine too.

Rowan's fingers at the nape of my neck. At first a tickling sensation. Then he squeezes my neck allowing me to know that he can squeeze a lot harder if he wishes.

He is excited explaining: Like them "out-top-sies" they do in a morgue. Y'know—"out-top-sie" with a human corpse you see in movies.

"Dis-mem-ber"—like cutting up a chicken, but with a special knife.

See, I brought my camera. I been taking some cool pictures. But I couldn't take any picture of myself.

Here's my camera, Jill-y, now you take some of me right here on this rock.

Know how it works? This button you press.

Look through the little lens. Then you press the button.

Don't pretend to be dumb, you're a fuckin smart little girl. Everybody says.

Hey Jesus!—watch out.

(The camera almost slips from my fingers into the creek, I am shaking so.)

Rowan snatches the camera from me, cursing.

Then seeing the sick scared look in my face, and laughing.

Seeing how I am gagging, and choking. Coughing up a thin frothy-white liquid onto the front of my shirt as Rowan Billict shakes his head and laughs.

What had it been, in the creek?—they are asking me.

What had Rowan Billiet brought me to see, and to take pictures of.

*Something that had drowned? Or been killed?
—shot?*

Carcass of a dog? A deer? A sheep?

In my life there are things *not-named*. If I shut my eyes I can see them clearly and yet they are *not-named*.

Waiting patiently for me to speak. Not police officers (I have been told) but social workers from Beechum County Family and Children's Services who are questioning me with my parents' approval (I have been told). I can feel how they pity me for it is easy to believe that I am slow-witted or so handicapped by shyness or by what has happened that it comes to the same thing as being slow-witted.

Overhearing one of them say to the others in a lowered voice *Maybe she just doesn't know. Maybe she never saw a thing but just imagined it. Maybe we are giving her ideas by asking these questions. . . .*

2.

Get a kick out of it.

More than once he'd said. Many times he'd said.

You'll get a kick out of it, Jill-y.

Winking at me like there's a joke between us. (What is the joke between us?)

But a *kick* is not a nice thing. You do not want to be *kicked*.

Or does *kick* mean that you will be doing the *kicking?*

But it is only a single *kick.* That is strange, I am thinking.

And years later, I still don't know. *Why would you think that a kick is a good thing?*

Thought you'd get a kick out of it, Jill-y.

Don't pretend you didn't. You did.

Bet you'd like to use my stained-steel Jap knife wouldn't you. Sure you would.

Next time, maybe you will.

Maybe a live thing. Hear him squeal.

Up at the road, at the sky-blue car I am still feeling shaky. My knees are weak. There's a buzzing in my head. The bad smell in my nostrils. Rowan scolds me if I'm gonna be puking in his car he don't want me in his car, I can walk back home.

Sounding disgusted with me but then he relents. Winks and laughs and says it's O.K. 'cause I'm just a girl and can't help it.

Feeling kind of sick and dazed but excited too. What I have seen has not entirely registered. It is easy to not-see it, to shut my eyes tight and wish all the ugliness away.

Thinking how there is this secret Rowan Billiet shared with me that makes me special even if I can't boast of it to my friends and girl cousins and no one will ever know.

Jill-y! You'll get a kick out of these.

In the glove compartment of the sky-blue Chevy smelling of kerosene and cigarette smoke are magazines Rowan Billiet keeps hidden he says except for special passengers.

Pulp-paper magazines Rowan Billiet shows me. Given to him by a friend (in Port Oriskany) he hopes I will meet someday. A friend who is a *colonel* (I think this is what Rowan says) who wants to meet me.

Why'd anybody want to meet *me*. This makes me laugh, it is so silly and improbable and scary.

Why'd any grown-up man like a "colonel" want to meet an eleven-year-old girl!

'Cause I told him about you, Jill-y. 'Cause I said you're my favorite niece and guess what the Colonel says?—he has no fuckin niece at all.

Rowan turns the magazine pages slowly. Wrinkled pages he smooths out on the car seat between us. *Police Files*, *True Detective*, *True Confessions*, *Argosy of Fear*, *FBI's Most Wanted*. Rowan's lower lip is caught in his small yellowish teeth. Rowan's shiny-glass eyes are fixed on me as I stare blinking at the faces in the magazines, the bodies in the magazines, of a kind I have never seen in the magazines that come into our house or on TV. These are bruised

24

and bloodied faces with shut eyes. These are bodies from which clothes have been removed or torn. Disfigured and deformed and mutilated bodies but it is clear that they are *female bodies* to which something terrible has been done.

Some girls are bad, Jill-y. They're "jail bait"— they "ask for trouble."

If a girl "asks for trouble"—y'know, she's gonna get it!

Did you ever see anything like this, Jill-y?

If I could speak I would tell him *no*.

Y'think you will ever look like her, Jill-y? When you're all growed up?

If I could speak I would tell him *no*.

She's biggern top than Irene, ain't she? But Irene has a nice ass not fat at all.

I don't like fat females. There's something disgusting about a fat ass when they sit on it, and it kind of *spreads*.

It's too bad what was done to this one, eh? Know what that's called?—where the knife cut her?

That's called a *nipple,* Jill-y.

You got them, too. Just little ones.

When you get older they get bigger. A lot bigger.

And if somebody pinches them—like this— they get *hard*.

Like Rowan is just playing, teasing. I pretend to think this. Pushing his hands away from my chest, giggling though his pinches hurt.

My eyes are aching at the corners and flooding with moisture so that I can't see what is on the page that Rowan has turned to.

Black Dahlia, they called her. Dirty girl got what she deserved.

Kind of cross-eyed ain't she? Slut.

Rowan's fingers gripping my hand. Rowan's forefinger and thumb gripping my wrist and tugging my hand toward him between his legs that are spread open at the knees.

Like this, Jill-y. Don't pretend to be dumb, you're a fuckin smart girl, Jill-y.

Rowan's breath is coming quick and sharp as if he has been running.

Rowan has removed the dark-tinted aviator glasses. His eyes are shiny like glass chips. His face is slick with sweat and the skin is a strange pale color like lard. His breath sounds as if it is hurting him.

There is a cry Rowan makes that is the cry of a small wounded animal. His eyes roll white in his head and a thread of saliva drops from his mouth.

Afterward Rowan says, If you ever tell any of this, Jill-y, your mother will know you for a bad, bad girl. Your father will whip your sweet little ass.

His bad luck, Rowan Billiet would say, he'd been born in Beechum County, New York. In L.A. he'd have had a chance—a career in popular music, movies, TV.

In L.A. you could be discovered in a drugstore, for instance. In Strykersville you would wait forever and not one good thing would ever happen to you.

He'd sent a glossy photo of himself to *The Dick Clark Show* identifying himself as a seventeen-year-old high school student with "dancing experience"—but he'd never heard back.

That was his luck, Rowan said. Born in Beechum County where there's a thousand times more cows than people.

In defiance of his surroundings Rowan Billiet was always well dressed! Nothing like the boys and men we knew.

Rowan Billiet was not a *manual laborer, worker.* He did not ever use his hands, he did not *dirty his hands* like other boys and men.

Instead, Rowan Billiet favored fresh-laundered white shirts, short-sleeved in summer. Sometimes a polka-dot bow tie. A belt with a silver or brass buckle.

His (short) legs in neat-ironed khakis or dark trousers. Not ever jeans or overalls—not for Rowan Billiet!

His jobs were always changing. No sooner did Rowan begin a job than he became restless, bored.

Drugstore clerk, shoe store salesman, ticket seller at the Starlite Drive-in. Busboy at Enzio's Pizza. At the Ransomville volunteer firemen's picnic in July Rowan Billiet was hired to call bingo numbers through a microphone in a smooth radio voice—*Ladies and gentlemen, BINGO!* These were mostly jobs you had to look nice for, nothing that would dirty Rowan's hands or clothing or muss his hair combed in a slick little pompadour like Elvis Presley's hair.

Rowan liked to boast he'd quit before he was fired. There were rumors he'd "helped himself to" merchandise or loose cash but Rowan Billiet was never arrested so far as anyone knew and my mother insisted that he had never stolen a penny in his life, Rowan had too much *dignity*.

At the time of Rowan's death it would be reported in the paper that he had no record of any adult arrest only traffic tickets and a summons.

Last job Rowan had was "private driver"—"chauffeur"—for a man named Cornel Steadman who lived in Strykersville. Mishearing his name people called Rowan's employer the Colonel.

Had to be the only chauffeur in Beechum County history, people said, sneering. For this position Rowan wore white shirt and bow tie, dark trousers, smart-looking hat with a dark green visor. Shiny black Cadillac de Ville he drove for the Colonel who sat sometimes in the rear of the vehicle and sometimes in the front seat beside Rowan Billiet.

On Main Street of Strykersville the men were seen in the Cadillac de Ville, frequently. The Colonel staring straight ahead like George

Washington crossing the Delaware River on Christmas Day 1776 (a reproduction of the painting hung in our school library) and beside him Rowan Billiet in chauffeur clothes and green-visor cap grinning and gripping the wheel tight.

The long black chrome-glittering automobile was impressive to see from the sidewalk but there were those (like my father) who identified it as a not-new Caddie, had to be ten years old at least.

The question would be put to me more than once: had Rowan Billiet ever driven me in the Cadillac? Had I ever ridden in the Cadillac with Rowan Billiet and Cornel Steadman? Had either man ever *touched me?*

There was a special emphasis to this word— *touched.* So that you knew that it meant more than it seemed to mean and that any answer to such a question had to be given with care.

No, I tell them.

Shaking my head so there is no confusion—*No.*

In fact I'd never glimpsed the Colonel. By the time Rowan Billiet knew the Colonel he'd forgotten me and he'd forgotten my mother who was his (step)-cousin he hadn't time for any longer.

Also I'd never glimpsed the shiny black Cadillac de Ville. So it is surprising to me, I seem to remember the beautiful car so clearly.

Shut my eyes and there it is and Rowan Billiet in the driver's seat sitting straight in his white shirt and bow tie, in tinted aviator glasses

and smiling at me like an arrow shot to my heart.
Jill-y! Make sure the fuckin door is shut.

Where did you drive with Rowan Billiet?
What kinds of things did Rowan Billiet say to you?
Did Rowan Billiet give you—gifts? Money?
Did Rowan Billiet show you—pictures? Photographs?
Did Rowan Billiet show you any of his knives?

Dismember was a word we had never heard. No child was told that word.

How old was I when I first heard the word *dis mem ber?*—it had to be after the day my father came to take me out of school. But when I try to remember it's like a blackboard that has been smudged.

Almost you can decipher the words or numerals beneath the smudge marks. You try and try until your eyes flood with tears from the strain but finally, you can't.

In the sky-blue Chevy he picks me up at the Greyhound bus station on Ferry Street, Strykersville, late on a rainy afternoon when the weather has changed. It is the day before Hallowe'en that would fall on a Friday that year.

It is almost dark at 5:15 p.m. Heavy bruise-color rain clouds have been blowing overhead all day.

I have told my mother that I am staying after school for basketball practice and I will catch the later (6 p.m.) bus home.

I am older now, I am in seventh grade at Strykersville Middle School. I don't remember how it has been arranged but it happens often in the fall of this year, Rowan Billiet picks me up at the bus station and drives me in his car out of town into the countryside when (it is believed by my mother) I am staying after school for *activities*.

Just at the edge of town there's a drive-in Dairy Queen where Rowan buys us milkshakes, sundaes, ice cream cones. And farther along State Highway 31 there's a tavern called The Pines that smells of beer and cigarette smoke and stale pretzels and something faintly sour and dank beneath.

It's like entering a cave. From the gravel parking lot into the tavern where Rowan Billiet says to the bartender *Hiya! Bud for me and Coke for my little niece.*

Rowan likes to empty his pockets on the bar. Jangling and jingly his spare change mixed with his car key.

The good thing is, Rowan gives me coins for the jukebox.

But today Rowan hasn't stopped at the Dairy Queen or The Pines. He hasn't stopped for a drink at the Iroquois Grill & Bowling Lanes where the proprietor is an old friend (Rowan says) of his father.

Instead he has driven out of Beechum County and into Monroe County through hilly countryside, pastures and fields now broken and desiccated with the stumps of cornstalks.

Turns into the Monroe Shopping Mall. This is a recently opened mall with more stores than you could imagine and a parking lot big as a football field.

Rowan is driving slowly now. As he drives he talks to me. As he talks to me he taps his fingers on the steering wheel in a staccato rhythm. I am not certain what Rowan is telling me but I like it that he calls me *Jill-y* which is a name no one else calls me.

His finger and thumb circling my wrist as no one else does.

Young children in masks and costumes are being escorted by their mothers into the shopping mall. Must be there's a Hallowe'en party tonight.

It is Devil's Night, when there is likely to be serious mischief committed by unsupervised teenagers.

Rowan brakes his car in little surges like hiccups. Moving at less than five miles an hour through the almost-empty parking lot. Dims his headlights out of courtesy.

Not all the costumed children are with adults,

it seems. Some appear to be with older children, hands grasped by older sisters or brothers.

Rowan brakes the car to a stop. Rowan has a surprise for me out of the glove compartment: a black satin half-mask to put on my face. And Rowan has a matching mask for himself.

Put it on, Jill-y!

The elastic catches in my hair as I adjust the mask on my face. The eye holes are not quite right for me to see through. The satin fabric is stiffer than you'd think.

But I like the mask, I like wearing the mask, peering at my reflection in the rearview mirror Rowan has shifted for me to look at.

Real sexy, Jill-y. Eh?

Rowan's black satin mask makes him look like the Devil in a cartoon drawing. Lower lip caught in his teeth in a wet sly grin.

Driving through the parking lot, slow. Rowan calls it *trolling*.

Like you *troll* for fish, if you are a fisherman.

But it is a very ugly sight, when a fish has swallowed a hook. When a fisherman yanks the squirming fish out of the water, and tears the hook out of the fish's bleeding mouth.

The fish eyes bulge. The fish gills open and close desperate to breathe.

There is a light chill rain. This is disappointing, on the night before Hallowe'en.

Rowan says, Look there, Jill-y.

Two girls my age. But I don't know them. The shopping mall is miles from Strykersville and in another school district.

The girls are only minimally dressed for Hallowe'en. The chubbier of the two is wearing a black crepe shawl in the design of a cobweb over black silky slacks like pajama bottoms. The other girl is wearing cheaply glamorous clothes including a "fox fur" boa and exaggerated makeup. Both girls have sequins sparkling in their hair and are wearing high-heeled shoes that cause them to walk awkwardly and bright red lipstick that makes their mouths glow unnaturally.

The girls are not very pretty, I am thinking. I wonder why they are not wearing masks.

Rowan whistles thinly through his teeth and I feel a twinge of jealousy—what's so special about *them?*

Rowan nudges me—Ask do they want a ride?

Because it's raining? It isn't raining hard. . . .

Jill-y! I said ask them.

This is not right. I shake my head *no.*

Just lean out the window. Ask if they want a ride. Say your dad will drive them wherever they want to go. . . .

Your dad. These words in Rowan's mouth are exciting to me.

But I am afraid to do this. Or I am reluctant to do this. For I am thinking—*This is not right. No.*

Yet I hate the girls, I think. They are older than

I am, probably fourteen or fifteen. They are *more mature* than I am and *sexy* in Rowan's eyes, I am sure.

I feel a twinge of anger at the girls. Just as Rowan is about to drive away I lower the car window and call out in a hoarse happy voice— Hi! D'you want a ride?

The girls turn to look at me. At the sky-blue Chevy, and Rowan Billict behind the wheel half his face hidden by the black satin mask.

It is scary to me, and it is exciting, to imagine what the girls are seeing when they look at us. When they look at me, in my black satin mask.

It's raining! Get in! My dad will drive you wherever you want to go. . . .

My voice is quavering. Even with the mask there is something in my face the girls can see, that causes them to shake their heads and smile nervously—No thanks!

You sure? It's no trouble—Rowan calls past my head.

His voice is a friendly voice. A friendly-dad voice.

But the girls are sure, they don't want a ride in the sky-blue Chevy driven by the smiling man in the black satin half-mask.

Their red-lipsticked lips are not smiling. Quickly they turn away in their high-heeled shoes.

In a whisper Rowan curses me. Terrible things

Rowan says to me, I can't believe that I am hearing.

You fucked up! You ugly little mutt! *You scared them off.*

Rowan drives the sky-blue Chevy joltingly through the parking lot. So angry he doesn't seem to know what he is doing.

Then, in silence along an adjacent road with steep drainage ditches on both sides.

By this time I have removed the black satin mask. It has fallen from my fingers onto the floor.

I am crying, and it is true, I know—my face is ugly when I cry.

Christ's sake. Listen to you.

In disgust Rowan brakes the car to a stop.

O.K. then, Rowan says. *Out.*

Rowan has also removed his mask and let it drop onto the floor at his feet. Leans across me and opens the door and pushes me out—so roughly, so unexpectedly, I am not able to comprehend what is happening.

It is such a surprise, I'm on my knees at the side of the road. Scrambling to get to my feet as Rowan drives away.

The red lights of Rowan's car, receding into the dusk!

My eyes are filled with tears of shock as well as hurt.

I am disbelieving. Rowan would not abandon

36

me here—would he? Isn't he my mother's cousin —step-cousin? Isn't he a relative of *mine?*

The road is a kind of service road beyond the shopping mall and seems to have no traffic. The diminishing red lights of Rowan's car are the only lights I will see.

The sky is a dull bruise color, heavy with rain clouds. In a few minutes it will be very dark.

I am sobbing uncontrollably. In the chill rain on this desolate road there is no one to hear.

Panicked wondering how I will get home. How many miles is it to the Cattaraugus Creek Road. Vaguely, desperately my mind races—if I can find my way back to the shopping mall . . . If I dared hitchhike on the state highway . . .

But I will never do this, I know. I am too shy. I am too frightened of what might happen to me, hitching a ride on the highway busy with out-of-state trucks.

I am so sorry! I would beg Rowan for forgiveness. I would promise him that I will never make such a mistake again, if he would forgive me.

Fucked up. Ugly little mutt. Don't deserve to live.

Rowan's jeering voice in my ears. Never will I forget this jeering voice.

Wanting so badly for Rowan to like me again. To laugh at me, tease me. Seize my wrist between his forefinger and thumb and call me a smart girl.

I would do anything for Rowan Billiet. I think again of the girls in the parking lot of the mall with bright lipsticked mouths and how they escaped from Rowan because I was not shrewd enough to stop them.

Next time! Next time I will do better.

And so by the time Rowan returns to rescue me I am ready to beg for his forgiveness.

There come glaring headlights out of the darkness, larger and larger until they are blinding. If it is not Rowan Billiet it will be a stranger who has come to murder me. . . .

I am crouched shivering beneath a tree near the drainage ditch that is beginning to fill with water.

It is Rowan, who throws open the passenger door of the sky-blue Chevy.

Saying in disgust, You! Jesus.

Like just the sight of me is repugnant to him.

Rowan's face isn't so handsome now contorted with dislike. His eyes show a rim of white above the iris like he'd really like to scream at me but is restraining himself. In a flat cold voice saying, Know what, Jill-y?—if you drowned right here, nobody'd ever know. And nobody'd give a God-damn.

But seeing how abject I am, how wet, muddy, abashed like a kicked dog, Rowan leans over to grab my wrist and haul me inside the car.

Not noticing, not caring, how rough he is, hurting my wrist.

Pleadingly I tell him, Next time I will do better, Rowan.

But Rowan snorts in derision. Presses down hard on the gas pedal without a further glance at me and turns the radio on high so there's just loud rock-and-roll music the rest of the way home.

3.

Forgive me, Rowan. I am so sorry!
Give me another chance please. . . .
But Rowan Billiet doesn't pick me up after school ever again.

Rowan Billiet doesn't drop by the house on one of his casual drives into the country to see if I'm home.

Can't ask my mother, What do you hear of Rowan? Any news?—because that would make her suspicious.

Climbing onto the roof of my grandfather's old barn. So that I can see into the distance past the front pasture to the creek road, and beyond.

If it's a sunny day the tin roof heats quickly. At first the heat is pleasurable beneath my legs and buttocks, then it becomes too hot, painful.

Any kind of hurt, you deserve. Ugly mutt.
I am sick with shame when I recall how Rowan Billiet is disgusted with me. It is very sad to think that Rowan has forgotten me. I am jealous that he may have found another girl-cousin to drive places in his sky-blue Chevy. (There are several

girl-cousins in our family, scattered through Beechum County.)

On the roof it is natural to think such thoughts. If I had the right kind of pride I would kill myself. I would find some way to put an end to myself. I would show Rowan Billiet how sorry I am, how ashamed I am. I would show Rowan Billiet that I disgust myself, too.

And Rowan Billiet would miss me then, and feel sorry he'd said the terrible things he said.

Jill-y! For Christ's sake I never meant it. You know better.

Know I care for you. C'mon climb in.

This time, do what I say. Exactly.

But Rowan Billiet never returns.

In two years by the time I am fourteen years old and a sophomore honors student at Strykersville High School Rowan Billiet is dead and the sky-blue Chevy is just one more vehicle tire-less and ransacked for parts in my uncle Mason Cutter's junkyard on the Cattaraugus Creek Road.

Here is what I know of Rowan Billiet.

It is put together like a jigsaw puzzle in which some puzzle parts are missing and some parts are not exact fits but have been forced into place so that the "picture" is not quite right if you look closely.

Yet it is a "picture" that makes sense. You can recognize what it is supposed to be.

Rowan was the son of a Beechum County woman who'd died at the age of thirty-one when Rowan was two years old. The woman had been separated from her husband at the time of her death as she'd been separated from her husband at the time of Rowan's birth. It was generally believed that her husband, who was my mother's older (half) brother Simon, was not the father of Rowan. Instead (it was believed) Rowan's father had been a man named *Billiet* about whom little was known.

Except Rowan's mother would say of him he was *the handsomest son of a bitch she'd ever seen.*

At that time in the early 1950s it was shameful if a woman had a baby without being married to the father of the baby. Extreme embarrassment and disapproval accrued to "illegitimate" births and so such situations were not spoken of with any clarity or openness to children nor even to teenagers; it was a time when breast, uterine, and cervical cancer were referred to as *mother's shame* and all medical problems related to women's reproductive organs were designated with vague distastefulness as *female problems.*

And so there were often misunderstandings. And these misunderstandings were rarely corrected because we (who were children or young adolescents at the time) had no way of knowing that there'd been misunderstandings.

Two things were known of the *Billiet* who was

believed to be the father of Rowan Billiet: there was no one else in Beechum County with that name; and the man with that name disappeared several months before Rowan was born.

My father did not like people to ask my mother about Rowan Billiet but even more, my father did not like my mother to speak of Rowan Billiet. It was strange to me that my father so disliked Rowan Billiet, he could not speak of him except in jeering and contemptuous terms—*That little fag.* It was very upsetting to my father to learn that some persons not well acquainted with our family believed that Rowan Billiet was related to *him.*

It has been many years since Rowan Billiet died yet people who should know better still make this mistake.

That uncle of yours, what was his name—Bill-yet? Your father's brother, was he? Or—who?

So maddening! You can't easily amend any misunderstanding in an individual's memory. Which is to say in the human brain.

Once a memory gets lodged in a brain even if the memory is inaccurate and has been disproven many times it will persist like an ineradicable stain.

Until the death of that brain, that is.

Pleading with my mother. Begging.

How badly I want to go to the volunteer firemen's picnic at Ransomville!

For I have learned that Rowan Billiet will be in charge of the bingo game. Rowan in a white shirt with a polka-dot bow tie. Sand-colored hair slicked over his forehead. His voice through the microphone slick like a radio voice. *Ladies and gentlemen, I think—I think—I THINK we have a winning card!*

I have not seen Rowan in a long time and this is my only opportunity and I am feeling desperate. . . .

My mother is astonished. Why do I want to bicycle to Ransomville to the firemen's picnic? Usually, I hate such picnics which are mostly for people with young children who clamor to be taken on noisy rides like a makeshift merry-go-round and a dwarf Ferris wheel and fat ponies flicking horseflies off their backs with their stinging tails. There are "games of skill" like throwing a baseball at some stupid target and there is the "chicken chowder tent" and there is the biggest tent of all which is the "beer tent" where men like my father stand crowded together and drink and talk and laugh loudly with flushed faces. *Since I'd been ten years old I have never wanted to attend such picnics with my family.*

But there is the bingo tent, too. Mostly women here, and girls, and older couples. And Rowan Billiet with the microphone.

But my mother has work for me today. Farm work I have put off doing.

Begging her: *Please, Mom.*

Just for an hour or two. *Please.*

I am pleading, reasonably: no one has to drive me to Ransomville. I don't expect my mother to get in the car and drive me. The distance is only about four miles, I can bicycle along the creek road.

Telling my mother in a whiny voice that my friends are all going. My friend Dina who lives in Ransomville . . .

My mother stares at me. *My friend Dina* is a girl I scarcely know, two years younger than me. Sometimes we ride together on the school bus just to avoid others. Hardly a close friend!

Also it is not like me to be so emotional. My mother is becoming suspicious.

I thought you hated these picnics. You always complain if you have to go. What's going on, Jill?

Nothing is *going on.* I just want to go to the picnic, that's all.

Why is this picnic so important?

My eyes flood with tears. I am suddenly so angry!

It is clear that in my mother's eyes there can be nothing in my life that is *so important.*

My face is flushed with heat, shame. I am in dread that my mother will realize—*It's Rowan Billiet she wants to see.*

And I am in dread that my mother will tell my father. That my mother will laugh, but my father will not laugh. That my father will be disgusted with me.

Billiet! That little fag.

I hope to hell he isn't coming out here and hanging around. If you want to see him, meet him in town for Christ's sake. If the little shit means so much to you, Jill.

I run away to hide. Run into the hay barn, and push through the rear window, to climb out onto the roof. Panting, half-sobbing. *Hate hatehate you!*

I wish that my mother was dead. I wish that Rowan Billiet would come to the house and murder her.

On the roof, my bare skin against the hot tin. In the distance there is farmland stretching out forever. The edge of the world looks hazy like it is melting away. I can't see all the way to Ransomville, I can't even see Cattaraugus Creek.

I don't even know whether Rowan Billiet is really in charge of the bingo tent this year. I don't know if I'd heard that somewhere, or read about it in the paper, or made it up.

After a long time I hear my mother calling from the far side of the barn—*Jill? Jill?*

I wonder if she feels sorry for having been so mean. I wonder if she realizes how I hate hatehate her and wish she was *dead.*

By now it is too late. It is almost 6 p.m. Of course she waited too long. She is spiteful, and she hates *me.* The time for bicycling to Ransomville (and back again) is over. Even if my mother now offers to drive me there it is too late.

And it is true as my mother has implied—nothing in my small sad stupid life is *so important.*

Questions never asked because the questioners from Beechum County Family and Children's Services lack sufficient information.

For instance: they do not know about the girls at the mall on Hallowe'en eve.

They do not know how Rowan Billiet pushed me out of his car on the desolate drainage-ditch road behind the mall.

Therefore they don't know to ask me why didn't I think of Rowan Billiet when news came in August 1962 of the missing eleven-year-old girl from Port Alistair, twelve miles north of Strykersville.

When news came in April 1963 of the missing thirteen-year-old girl from Tintern Falls, eight miles east of Strykersville.

When news came a few weeks later of the *remains discovered in a shallow grave . . .*

Why didn't I tell someone. My mother at least.

Why wasn't I suspicious.

Was I suspicious?

And if so, why did I remain silent?

I could say—*Because I was afraid of Rowan Billiet.*

I could say—*Because Rowan Billiet threatened me.*

Some of this is true, I was afraid of Rowan Billiet.

But it is not true, I think, that Rowan Billiet threatened me.

In fact it is likely, Rowan Billiet would never have hurt *me.*

And why is this?—because Rowan Billiet liked to speak of himself as my *uncle,* and sometimes my *dad.*

Even when Rowan was furious with me, and disgusted with me, still he *was fond of me.*

This I know. It is a (secret) memory I cherish.

In the papers and on TV Rowan Billiet was described as *Local Strykersville Man, 27.*

Which was strange to me, that Rowan Billiet was considered to be a *man;* and that he had an actual age, *twenty-seven.*

Rowan Billiet did not seem any age at all. To some of us who knew him he did not ever seem that old.

When you are thirteen years old, or even fourteen or fifteen, twenty-seven is *old.*

Almost we wanted to think that was a mistake. My girl friends who'd seen Rowan Billiet and thought he was *real good-looking, handsome like Elvis.*

If you'd asked us we would've guessed Rowan was—what? Twenty-one years old, *maybe.*

Another wrong thing, Rowan Billiet did not live in Strykersville exactly. It was known that he lived in different places in Beechum County and never the same place for long. Once (my mother recalled) with some "hippie" people on the Canal Road in an old falling-down farmhouse. (My mother disapproved.) Another time with relatives in the Rapids and later, in the last several months of his life, with the older man (who did live in Strykersville, in one of the big brick houses on Ridge Avenue) who was called *the Colonel* (a mishearing of the name *Cornel*).

In Cornel Steadman's house on Ridge Avenue, in the room that was Rowan Billiet's room, there would be discovered a "cache" of incriminating evidence—articles of clothing belonging to the murdered/dismembered girls, dozens of snapshots taken with Rowan Billiet's Kodak camera and neatly pasted into a photo album.

These snapshots the police would confiscate as evidence that would help to incriminate Rowan Billiet posthumously.

Posthumously meaning that by this time, Rowan Billiet was himself dead, murdered and "dismembered."

(Though there were some who believed that Cornel Steadman placed the incriminating snapshots in Rowan's room after he'd murdered Rowan.)

(Why did Cornel Steadman murder and

dismember Rowan Billiet?—this was not clear. A theory was that Steadman was jealous of Rowan who'd threatened to leave him.)

Police used these snapshots to determine that the thirteen-year-old girl missing for eight months from Tintern Falls had been buried in a region of the Chautauqua Mountains where a certain species of ash tree is predominant, which led to their discovering her (dismembered) remains there.

All of Rowan Billiet's possessions they would confiscate. All of Cornel Steadman's possessions. In fact Cornel Steadman's entire house was declared a *crime scene.*

Later, the house was sold at auction. The mortgage had been *foreclosed* by a Strykersville bank where one of my mother's old, close friends from high school was a teller.

You can drive by it today—838 Ridge Avenue.

Someone lives in the old three-story redbrick house with the steep slate roof but it looks as if often they are not home. Blinds are drawn on windows upstairs and down. The front lawn has gone to seed. Newspapers and flyers have accumulated on the front walk. One of the big old elms in the side yard was devastated in a windstorm and has split in two.

My mother would never drive by the house she says with a shudder is a *haunted house.* My father has said disgustedly *Somebody should burn that place down.*

4.

Here is what I know, that I have been told. Or that I have heard without being told.

In Port Oriskany they'd met, at the Niagara Inn, Rowan Billiet and Cornel Steadman—the Colonel.

The Colonel would be forty-nine years old at the time of his arrest by the Beechum County police. In his pictures he was stern-looking with a stark bald head and dark dyed-looking hair above his ears, heavy eyebrows and fat fleshy lips. The Colonel looked like somebody you have seen on TV, his face is that kind of face.

For eight months or so, Rowan Billiet was the Colonel's *chauffeur*.

Rowan Billiet lived in the Colonel's house on Ridge Avenue, which the Colonel had purchased in order to move away from Port Oriskany where the Colonel complained of having enemies.

The men began to travel together. To "take trips together."

In the shiny black Cadillac de Ville that Rowan Billiet drove.

These were "day trips" to other regions of New York State like the Chautauqua Mountains or the Adirondacks—or "out-of-state" trips to Pennsylvania, Ohio, even Ontario (Canada).

(Where was the sky-blue Chevy at this time?

Left behind in the three-car garage at the Colonel's house where police would discover it. Somehow the Chevy was dented by now, with rusted chrome and a worse-stained back seat. Bloodstains and clumps of hair on the floor of the trunk. And the chassis not so *sky-blue* as we remembered.)

The men had been to Vegas several times. It was "Vegas" and not "Las Vegas" to them.

The Colonel spoke proudly of himself as a *professional poker player*. Rowan Billiet favored blackjack and boasted that he'd been asked to leave several casinos because he had *figured out the game*.

When the men went to Vegas they flew business class, and left the Cadillac behind.

In Vegas, they would rent a vehicle. It was crucial, the Colonel said, to always have a vehicle *at your disposal*.

After the discovery of Rowan Billiet's remains car rentals in Vegas contracted by Cornel Steadman would be studied carefully. Mileage on the cars would be examined, and credit card receipts.

There was an unsolved abduction of a ten-year-old boy from Carson City, Nevada, in February 1962. This was at a time when Rowan Billiet and Cornel Steadman had been in Vegas registered (in a suite) at the Mandalay Bay Hotel and Casino; Cornel Steadman had rented a car for six days. The boy had disappeared from the back yard of his suburban home two miles from downtown Vegas and was never seen again. His abductor or abductors had not asked for ransom. Though searchers had made their way on foot through much of Ormsby County, Nevada, no trace of the body had ever been found.

If I try to remember the last time I saw Rowan Billiet a cloud comes over my brain. I don't want to think it was when Rowan shoved me out of his car and called me *ugly mutt* so I try to remember an earlier time when Rowan smiled at me and circled my wrist with his forefinger and thumb and praised me for being *a fuckin smart little girl.*

My mother says she just can't remember when she saw her (step)-cousin last. Shuts her eyes like she's feeling dizzy, and presses the back of her hand against her forehead.

Oh. Damn Rowan. Never one you could *rely on.*

One day at school there came a message for me. I will never forget fourth-period geometry and a knock at the door and it was requested that I bring my books with me and go to the principal's office. And everybody stared after me—including the teacher. My heart knocking so hard against my ribs, I could almost not move my legs. And downstairs my father was waiting with this look in his face like he'd been hit over the head with a mallet. And it was a terrible thing, that my father was not at work at the GM factory, so that I knew that someone had died and I was very frightened.

Jill! C'mon.

My father just grabbed my arm and pulled me. The principal was trying to talk to him, or had been talking to him, but as soon as my father saw me he grabbed me and walked me out of the building with him like he wasn't even hearing the principal, had forgotten the principal entirely.

It was like my father to be rude sometimes. But it was not like my father to be rude to another man, especially a man who was wearing a suit, a white shirt and a necktie and eyeglasses.

In the car I was trembling badly. I could not speak. For I knew that my mother had died, and that it was my fault for I had wished that my mother would die. I was sick with this knowledge. I did not even ask my father how my mother had died, or where she was when she'd died. Or where he was taking me now.

My father was saying to me in a low angry surprised-sounding voice that it was better to take me home now, before the news was *all over town.*

All over town—I could see this. Shut my eyes and it was a flock of black-feathered birds flapping their wings *all over town.*

But it was not my mother who had died. It was not my mother whose *remains* had been found in an *abandoned quarry.*

And so it was a great relief to me not to be at school on the day that Rowan Billiet's picture was on the front page of the *Strykersville Journal.*

It was a bad shock but also a relief, I would not have to run away to hide in a girls' restroom.

Still it would be hard for me to face my close girl friends who knew that Rowan Billiet was a relative of mine, and someone special to me.

It was revealed that Rowan Billiet had been "missing" for approximately eight weeks. (Had I known this? Had my mother known this? We had not seen Rowan in so long it was like this awful thing had happened to a stranger.) The body had been found by hikers in an abandoned limestone quarry at Iron Forge, in the Chautauqua Mountains. This was about seventy-five miles southwest of Strykersville.

The body had been *dismembered* with something like a sharp ax or special knife. The parts had been *scattered*. Coyotes, foxes, possibly dogs and vultures had been scavenging at the site. It was my father who had to make the identification at the Beechum County Morgue for my mother could not have done this and other relatives (it seemed) were too old, or too feeble, or too upset, or too disgusted and just flatly refused. So ironically it was my father who'd had to identify the remains of Rowan Billiet, who would have to insist for the rest of his life that Rowan Billiet was no relative of his and only "remotely related" to my mother.

My father was not a softhearted man but he returned to the house stricken, very quiet.

People would ask my father why he'd been the one to identify Rowan Billiet's *remains* when there'd been others who might have done it, or should have done it, and my father said with a pained look and a shrug of his shoulders, Jesus! I don't know.

I guess, it was the least I could do. Seeing that he's Irene's cousin or whatever the hell he was.

My mother did not ask my father what he'd seen at the county morgue. My mother did not ask as others did *Who would do such a terrible, sick thing* for (gradually I came to realize) my mother was not so surprised.

I have not mentioned that my mother had a pretty turquoise necklace that Rowan Billiet had given her a year or so before his death. Just aqua glass meant to be "turquoise" and fake-gold for (my mother said) Rowan had probably found the necklace in a tavern or on the ground somewhere, picked it up and put it in his pocket and the first person he happened to run into, in town, to whom he might give such a necklace, was my mother.

My mother laughed saying it was typical of her cousin, to hand over such a "gift," not even noticing that the necklace had long thin hairs caught in the glass beads, that must have belonged to the owner.

(But what became of the turquoise necklace from Rowan Billiet? When police made inquiries my mother did not mention it. To me she'd said more than once that the necklace had been lost and it was true, I never saw it again.)

Everyone who knew him said of my father that he was never the same person after the identification of Rowan Billiet at the county morgue. If a body has been *dismembered* you would "identify" only the head, the face. But if the head is not attached to a torso? To a neck? You'd see my father staring off into a corner of the room. He'd become a distracted person. He rarely laughed, and his old way of laughing and jeering had ended. In the midst of a conversation he'd go suddenly quiet. Set down whatever it was he'd been drinking, and you would know what he was thinking about, what he was remembering.

Except you hadn't seen it, and so you didn't really know.

Dis member.

If you say this word aloud it will sound like *re mem ber.*

Dismember was not a word we had been told.

Dismember is a word that sticks in your head like a burr or a thorn in clothes.

As soon as the police came for him the Colonel confessed. Led the police up the stairs to Rowan Billiet's room and told them *Everything is here. Not a thing has been hidden. I've been waiting for you, gentlemen.*

Together they had killed the two girls, the Colonel said. He and his chauffeur Rowan Billiet.

The Colonel knew of details that had been known only to the police, that had not been printed in any newspapers. And he claimed there'd been other girls and "a boy or two" they had abducted, killed, dismembered, and buried in other states including Nevada.

Why'd they do such terrible things, the Colonel was asked; and the Colonel replied it hadn't been his idea but Rowan Billiet's.

See, the Colonel said, Rowan liked the thrill of cutting up a body—*disarticulating*. To hear the Colonel speak of it he'd been totally in the power of the younger man.

He'd had to kill Rowan Billiet, the Colonel claimed, to keep Rowan Billiet from killing more children.

It was the only way, the Colonel insisted. Also, he'd had to kill Rowan Billiet to keep Rowan Billiet from killing *him*.

This caused a sensation in Beechum County!— in all of western New York State. The Colonel's "confession" was in all the papers and on TV.

Rowan's relatives protested—there was no way for Rowan to defend himself!

My mother was devastated by Rowan's murder. My mother did not believe a word of the Colonel's confession except that he'd killed Rowan in cold blood. She did not believe that her (step)-cousin Rowan had ever killed anyone, she knew Rowan and *he was not like that.*

It was this sick, terrible man who'd murdered and dismembered children and was lying now to incriminate poor Rowan who was one of his victims, who could not defend himself.

Cornel Steadman pleaded guilty to several counts of first-degree homicide and was sentenced to death in the electric chair. But he was never executed, only just died in prison in Attica of heart failure at the age of sixty-two.

It is true, when a dead man is accused of terrible crimes, he cannot defend himself.

Among the snapshots in Rowan Billiet's room were a number of snapshots of a young girl identified as *Jill Cotter.* Some of them had been taken at the creek that day, and some other days (that I had forgotten).

And so, I was one of those persons "interviewed" by authorities.

Most of what I said is *I don't remember.*

I wish that I could help you but I don't remember.

Or I would say *I don't know! Leave me alone.*

After approximately a week the questions ceased. During this period of time my clothes grew loose on my body, my mother was appalled when I lost eight pounds. Neither she nor my father asked me questions about Rowan Billiet. Girls at school were the ones to ask me but I shook my head rudely, I had nothing to say to them.

Silence has gathered around me like a thick, viscous water filling in a muddy footprint.

Early evening, swollen sky like an eye that is shut, that has been blinded. On the slanted roof, just slightly sagging, of my grandfather's old barn, where the heat of the tin beats against my bare legs, thighs.

This is a forbidden place. If an adult sees me I will be scolded harshly—*Jill, get down! You know better.*

It is true, I know better. I am not a young child any longer.

I am long-limbed, lanky. I am a senior at Strykersville High School. I have many friends but in truth, of course I have no friends. I am known as a "witty"—"articulate"—"secretive" person. I am an honors student—of course. Sometimes I write about Rowan Billiet on sheets of lined notebook paper, then I crumple the pages without reading them and throw them away.

Rowan Billiet would be surprised to see me now, maybe he would not recognize me.

I think that I am better-looking now. I am not so ugly, I think.

To look at, I am not so ugly.

The roof of my grandfather's barn, the side that faces farmland, and not the house, is a special place for me.

Refuge is a word for it. One of those adult words that contain more meanings than you can say simply.

I am the only girl my age who continues to climb on this roof that is obviously an unsafe roof. The tin sheets are rusty, and sagging. Inside the barn, when it is raining there is a staccato pelt of raindrops like bullets.

By eighth grade we'd mostly lost interest in my uncle's junked vehicles as well.

You forget. You lose interest. Other things to do.

Things you did as a child, even forbidden things you disdain when you are a few years older.

He's driving his Chevy along Iron Road. Bright sky-blue with chrome fixtures that gleam like winking eyes. In a few miles he will turn onto the Cattaraugus Creek Road which is our road and in a few minutes shading my eyes I will see the blue car moving swiftly in my direction.

Jill-y! When's your birthday?

What would you like for your birthday, Jill-y?

Could be, I will have a surprise for you.

THE CRAWL SPACE

Please. You make us uncomfortable.

You are always watching us. Like a ghost haunting us . . .

Though her husband had died seven years before the widow still drove past the house in which they'd lived for more than two decades.

Why?—no reason.

(To lacerate a scar, that it might become a raw-throbbing wound again? To lacerate her conscience? *Why?*)

She was in a new life now. She was no longer in the old life.

He could not know. He had died, his ashes were buried in a proper cemetery. All that was gone. In her new, safe life, in which she lived alone.

Yet: sometimes she drove past the old house deliberately, and sometimes she found herself driving past without (quite) realizing where she was. Then, it was something of a shock to see— where she was. . . .

Often when she was driving she would instruct herself *Maybe no. Not today.* And yet when she approached a crucial turn she found herself unable to drive onward as if doing so would be a

61

betrayal of her husband whom she had loved very much.

As he had loved her. *Very much.*

Similarly, she felt the same way while driving through the small town in which her husband's ashes were buried—in a cemetery behind an old redbrick Presbyterian church, that dated to the mid-nineteenth century.

She could not not stop at the cemetery. Could not.

Just us two. No one else.

Very much.

Of course, she understood how mistaken this was. No force was compelling her to drive past her former house, or to stop in the little town, that was losing population and becoming derelict since an interstate highway bypass opened close by.

Its sad Main Street, with vacant stores. For Sale signs. The small cemetery in need of mowing, at this time of year festooned with dandelions gone to seed.

The widow parks at the cemetery, she visits the husband's grave. *It is only my own mind. It is not another's mind, that is making me do these things.*

Still, she clears away leaves and other debris from the grave. Sets upright the ceramic pot containing the (artificial) wisteria with its sinewy vines and lavender blossoms she'd brought to the grave, that has been surprisingly durable through winter months. Almost, you would think the blossoms were real. . . .

A small enough gesture from you, my beloved wife. But thank you.

She did not like it: they were watching her.

She was certain. The new owners of the house. For she so often drove past the house.

At more rational times she thought no, of course not. The new owners—(whom she'd met: they were nice-seeming people)—would have to be standing at the front windows of the house and looking out at just the time she drove past. They would have to recognize her car.

Yet, approaching the house she begins to feel her heartbeat quickening. A visceral alertness of the kind you might feel approaching the edge of a great height. Vertigo, it is called. A sensation of dread, and yet yearning. You dare not approach—yet, you are drawn to approach. Almost, you feel an opened hand on the small of your back, gently pushing.

Come here! Come forward.

Yes! You know exactly what to do.

The new owners had assured her, out of sympathy for her widowhood (she'd supposed), that, any time she wished, she could come back to visit the house. They'd been very friendly, very kind-seeming, but she'd never wanted to return to the house, in any way that involved them. Though she knew better she could not help but think of them as intruders whom she resented, and whom she knew her husband, who could be unreasonable, would most bitterly resent.

So many years she'd driven this route: returning to the house on Linden Road which was five miles from the small suburban college at which she taught English; turning her car into the asphalt driveway; feeling anticipation as she approached the house, unless it was apprehension—for she never (quite) knew what her husband's mood would be.

Nearly always, the husband was home. For the husband did consulting work in applied mathematics, working from an office at home.

Not wanting to think *Like clockwork* for, living our lives, as our bodies live for us, we are not at all clockwork; we do not feel ourselves to be clockwork; each second is new to us, quicksilver and unexpected, undefined.

Unexpected: that day she'd returned home, not from the college but from the medical clinic. With the news that had shaken them both.

Him more than her. For he'd been the one who'd most adamantly not wanted a child.

In his family, mental derangement. (As he called it.) Not mental illness, insanity or psychosis—nothing that could be clinically diagnosed, or treated. Just—*derangement.*

She, the wife, a young wife at the time, had not wanted to inquire too closely. She saw the pain in her husband's handsome thin-cheeked face. She saw that he was distressed, and anxious.

He'd carried himself with a sort of sinewy muscularity, a physical obstinacy that didn't express his scrupulosity, his fastidiousness. He'd been a perfectionist, and had driven himself very hard in graduate school; from rueful remarks he'd made, she understood that he had come close to a nervous breakdown, or perhaps had actually had a nervous breakdown before he'd met her, and he did not want to risk anything like this again.

What is *manliness, masculinity?*—she felt sympathy for her husband, for whom imperfection was a kind of shame. She did not like to pry into his personal life, which he called "private."

Still, she'd thought that, possibly, *mental derangement* might not be such a risk. . . .

He'd reacted almost violently: No.

No pregnancy. Must terminate. We can't. Can't take the chance. What if. No.

But—

No. I've told you.

Can't risk.

Even if the child is—is not—abnormal. Even then—

Our own lives. Must come first.

What we mean to each other.

She'd done as he had instructed. Or rather, as he'd demanded.

Thinking—*It is what I want, too. Of course.*

Emotionally, the husband was the center of her life. Her professional career was not very challenging to her: she had no wish to compete strenuously, and to excel; she was highly competent, reliable and well liked. At her small suburban college it was not difficult to be promoted to the highest professorial rank and to decline (when, more than once, it was offered to her) advancement into administration. Her salary was not high but it supplemented her husband's salary to a degree that made them financially secure.

We can afford a child. Children.

She did not say. Did not risk.

(Perhaps) (she was thinking) it was a mistake to have moved into a place not far from the old house when her husband died. She'd had to sell the house—of course. Soon after his death which had been an unexpected death after a brief, virulent illness. In a state of grief and exhaustion she'd looked at a number of possible places in which to live nearer the college yet somehow she'd found nothing quite right, and decided to rent a condominium hardly a mile from the old house on Linden Road.

And so, approaching her former house as she'd approached it for so many years, sometimes alone in her car, sometimes beside her husband in the driver's seat—(for always Jed drove when she was with him in the car: he would never have allowed anyone else to drive)—she could not overcome a sense of apprehension though she knew, of course she knew, that the house belonged to strangers, and that (probably!) these strangers were not standing vigilant at their front windows waiting for the widow to pass by. Yet still, her heartbeat quickened as she approached: in her mind's eye she parked her car as usual in front of the garage, and made her way from the car into the small flagstone courtyard, and opened the front door which was painted a deep ruby-red, and stepped inside—*Hello? I'm home. . . .*

The husband had not liked it if, as she'd done sometimes, she entered the house without announcing her arrival. Hoping for a few minutes to herself, private time, to catch her breath (she might've said), put a few groceries away in the kitchen which she'd picked up on the way home, before calling to her husband—*Hello, Jed. It's me.*

Sometimes, if Jed was home, and he'd heard her, he would come to greet her; more often, she would seek him out in his office, which was a large, comfortable room at the rear of the house on the second floor.

Once, when a late-afternoon meeting was canceled and she'd returned to the house earlier than Jed expected her, the door had been locked against her. The doors.

She'd tried the front door—locked. Thinking it was just an accident, she tried another. Locked.

And another—also locked.

Of course, she should have had a house key. What was the reason she hadn't had a house key?

He was nearly always home. His car was in the driveway now. She'd lost the habit of taking a house key with her and so, after a moment's hesitation, she knocked on the door, not loudly, not rudely, for she did not want to disturb the husband if he was in deep concentration at his work, but still there was no answer and (so far as she could see) no movement inside the house.

She walked around the house, peering in windows. "Jed? *Jed?*"

Had to be upstairs. Maybe playing music, wearing earphones.

(Why was she so agitated? Her underarms stung with perspiration, a rivulet of sweat ran down the side of her face like an errant tear.)

(But he was alone, she was sure. He had never brought anyone to the house in her absence. She was sure.)

"Jed? It's me. . . ."

Each of the doors was locked. Pride prevented her from checking the windows.

The solution came to her—*I will go away as if this has not happened. No one will know.*

It was an era before cell phones. But if she'd

called, she had the idea that her husband would not have answered the phone.

She went away. She returned hours later, at the expected time. All the doors were unlocked. Interior lamps had been lit. When she entered the house he was awaiting her with a little bouquet of Shasta daisies, carnations, and red rose buds.

"For you, dear. Missed you."

She was touched. She was relieved. She smiled happily, as a young bride might smile, sweetly naïve, trusting. She kissed his cheek and asked as it would have been natural for a young bride to ask, "But why? Today is not a special day, is it?"

"No day with you is not a special day, darling."

He had shaved, his lean jaws were smooth and smelled of lotion. His white cotton shirt was fresh. The sleeves were rolled to the elbows as he rarely, perhaps never wore them.

Later, when the husband was elsewhere and would not discover her, she'd examined his office. His closet in their bedroom. Their bed.

Cautiously lifted the bedclothes to stare at the lower sheet that (so far as she could judge) was smoothed flat as it had been when, that morning, she'd briskly made up the bed.

What on earth am I looking for? she was ashamed, she had no idea.

What has he made me into, how has this happened. How is this person—me?

In marriage, one plus one is more than the sum of two. But sometimes in a marriage, one plus one is less than the sum of two.

He was correct: it would not have been worth the risk.

She'd come to agree. Their very special feeling for each other, their unique love, would have been irrevocably altered by the intrusion of another.

Seven years! The time has passed quickly; or, the time has passed very slowly.

There have been few changes to the house, that she can see from the road. But there had been changes.

When she drives past the house she finds herself slowing the car, to stare. Her heart quickens in anticipation of seeing something that will upset her.

She hates it, seeing changes in her former house that upset her!—thinking how these changes would upset her husband, too.

For some reason the new owners removed the redwood fence which the husband had had erected at the front of the property, for privacy. (Why on earth? Had the fence become rotted? She didn't think so.)

Then, they'd had the house repainted: a dull beige with brown shutters so much less striking than the original cream with dark red shutters.

Once, seeing that the new owners had had a

large oak tree removed from the front lawn, she'd felt weak with indignation. She'd happened to drive past at the time of the tree's demise, chain saw rending the air into unbearable shards of sound. Screaming.

He had not screamed at his fate. Rather, he'd been medicated, unable to protest. He had not even known (she'd wanted to think) what was happening in his body. That sequence of small, inexorable surrenders.

In fact, yes: he had screamed at his fate. He'd screamed at her.

Not that he'd known who she was, then. Not that he'd hated *her.*

Slowly she drove in the tense delirium of approach. For it seemed to her—*Of course, I am going home. It's an ordinary evening.*

(But why then was she so frightened? The *ordinary* does not provoke fear.)

He hadn't been comfortable with the *ordinary,* in fact. His work had been a highly refined mathematics applied to the manufacture of digital equipment which she hadn't understood even when he'd tried to explain to her in the plainest speech.

He hadn't been comfortable with *resting.* He hadn't taken a vacation in the more than twenty years she'd known him. At one time he'd worked as many as one hundred hours a week as a consultant for (rival) companies. She felt a thrill of horror that, now that he'd died, he could not ever do anything meaningful again. *That* would have hurt him, stung his pride.

How surprised he'd have been to see a stranger so comfortable in his house. At his worktable, a long white table, wonderfully practical, useful. *What is this? What has happened?* In his bed.

How like science fiction our lives are, she thinks. The alternate universe in which, innocently, ignorantly, we continue to exist as we'd been, unaware that, in another universe, we have ceased to be.

Without knowing what she has done, the widow has parked the car on Linden Road in front of the house.

Oh but *why!* She'd meant to drive past.

She thinks—*But I am safe now. I can't be hurt now. I am alive now. I am not sick now.*

After her husband died she'd been sick for some time. An actual sickness, shingles. A sickness of the heart, heartsickness, that had almost killed her.

Where are you, I am waiting for you. God damn you—have you betrayed me.

She had not! She had not betrayed him.

Dreams of wading into a river. Swimming a river, her arms and legs like lead. Dreaminess of surrender to the leaden river, that drew her down, to dreamless sleep.

It's about time. Seven years! Rats are more faithful than you.

"Hello—?"

She hears a voice, unfamiliar, yet friendly-seeming, as she stands in the roadway, uncertainly. It is strange—she doesn't remember having left her car. . . .

In the asphalt driveway of the former house a woman is standing, waving to her. This must be Mrs. Edrick, whom she'd met seven years before when she'd sold the house through a broker.

How embarrassing! And there is another person, a man, the husband probably, in the background.

They have sighted her. She must acknowledge them now. The friendly-seeming woman is coming to speak to her.

Please. You make us uneasy.

You are always driving past our house. You are always watching us. We hate it, you are a ghost haunting our lives.

How stricken she would be, if the Edricks spoke to her in this way! She is feeling breathless as if under attack.

But Mrs. Edrick does not utter these hostile words. Mrs. Edrick is smiling pleasantly at her. The woman is just slightly younger than she, and stands with her arms folded across her chest as if cold. At a little distance, Mr. Edrick is standing hesitantly as if uncertain whether to come forward, or retreat back into the house as husbands sometimes do in such circumstances.

"Hello! Is it—Brenda?"

"Brianna."

" 'Bri-anna.' Yes. It's been a while since we've spoken. How are you?"

The question seems bold, even aggressive. *How is she?*—she is a widow.

"I—I'm well. I'm sorry if I . . ."

"Oh no, not at all! We would have called but we'd misplaced your number. We see you sometimes driving past our house—that is, your former house—and thought we'd have an opportunity to tell you: there seem to be things of yours still in the house, of which you're probably not aware."

Of which you're probably not aware. The formality of the woman's speech suggests that it has been planned, rehearsed. The widow sees now that there is something steely and resolute in the woman's smiling face.

Things of yours still in the house. This is the crucial statement. She feels a jolt of apprehension, and yet hope.

"At least we think it must belong to you, Brianna, or to your late husband. Several boxes . . ."

Mrs. Edrick explains that a furnace repairman had recently come to the house and discovered, in the crawl space, several boxes taped shut with black duct tape that seemed to have been there for some time.

Crawl space. A sinister term, she'd thought it. Her husband had stored things in the basement, in the "crawl space," which he hadn't wanted to discard but didn't think he needed to access any longer: boxes of old receipts, checks, IRS records, expired warranties and miscellaneous documents. All she'd ever seen of the "crawl space" was its opening, at a height of about four feet, in one of the dank basement walls; her husband had managed to crawl inside, to leave boxes there, but she'd never felt any curiosity about exploring it.

What was the purpose of a crawl space in a house, she'd asked her husband, and he'd said he supposed it was for extra storage, and for the use of workmen who needed to access parts of the basement otherwise out of reach: electricians, for instance.

Pleasantly smiling Mrs. Edrick leads Brianna into the kitchen. (Quickly Brianna sees that the kitchen, her former kitchen, is both familiar and utterly strange: have the new owners repainted the walls? Is the ceiling no longer white, but an oppressive beige? The tile floor, richly dark-russet-red when she'd lived here, is now a busy and unattractive swirl of pinpoint colors. A wall of cupboards seems to have disappeared.) "Here you are!"—Mrs. Edrick is handing her a soiled-looking shoe box taped shut with black duct tape. "The repairman brought this box upstairs, it's the smallest. He says there are two or three larger boxes still there. We'd been meaning to contact you—we hope the boxes don't contain anything too important."

Was this *rude?* Brianna wonders.

But no, obviously not. Not intentionally rude.

Quickly she says, "Yes—I mean no, I'm sure the boxes don't contain anything—important." She is speaking hesitantly, staring at the box, which exudes an air of subtle, indefinable menace.

(What could Jed have stored in a box this size? Nothing out of the ordinary, surely. Financial records, check stubs? Letters?)

(But what sort of letters, hidden away in a crawl space in a taped-over shoe box?)

How excessively intricate, the taping! Brianna recalls how carefully, over-carefully, her husband had taped packages for the mail. Taking his time, as if he'd enjoyed the simple methodical process, *taping shut.*

Her eyelids flutter. A sudden vision, as in a surreal film, of a human face, small, possibly a child's face, black tape covering mouth, eyes.

What is best. Don't question.

On the box is a badly faded label, hand-printed in the husband's distinctive hand: 12 Feb. 2009. No other identification. She recalls the stately old Parker fountain pen he'd had. An artifact from another era, a father's or a grandfather's pen, that required liquid ink.

After the husband's death, the pen had disappeared.

"Oh, dear!—I hope the box wasn't waterlogged. We had a little flood in our basement from all the rain, last spring. . . ."

"Oh yes. We did, too."

(But why does the widow say *we?* She lives alone in the rental property a mile away, there is no longer any *we*.)

In a confiding-neighbor voice Mrs. Edrick says: "We keep all sorts of things, too. In the garage mostly. It's terrible, how things accumulate in our lives as if they had a life of their own. . . ."

The widow murmurs agreement. She has no idea what Mrs. Edrick is chattering about. Her eyes well with tears, Mrs. Edrick is politely not acknowledging.

Weighing the soiled shoe box in her hand. Yes, probably papers.

Letters. (Love letters?)

(But there were no love letters exchanged between the widow and her husband who'd never spent any time apart after they'd met.)

Her breath is coming short. Every particle of her being is crying out in astonishment—*How is this possible, is this something my husband has left for me? Or is it something my husband did not ever intend for me?*

She feels a moment's vertigo. Paralysis. She has taken the shoe box from Mrs. Edrick but it is very heavy—she has had to set it down on a table.

Feeling the other woman's eyes on her. The husband has approached silently, behind her; the Edricks have exchanged an indecipherable look.

Almost palpable, their pleas tinged with impatience, anger.

Please go away. Leave this house. Do not haunt us—no more!

But again Mrs. Edrick appears to be very friendly. Seeing the expression in the widow's face of something like pain, and yet yearning, she says, "Brenda—I mean Brianna—if you'd like, you can examine the crawl space yourself. You have our permission! The furnace repairman said there were at least two more boxes. He might have dragged them out if I'd asked him, but I didn't think to ask, at the time. And neither of us"—(Mrs. Edrick is referring now to her husband, whose face Brianna has not seen)—"is especially eager to crawl into such a space."

The widow is feeling disoriented. She recognizes the sensation—heightened excitement, apprehension—a curious mixture of fear and hope—an intensification of the way she invariably feels when she drives by the former house. And now, so suddenly, with no preparation she is standing *in the former house.*

What has brought her here? Has it been—*him?*

Certainly, she does not want to descend into

the basement! Not into the crawl space!—which she remembers as grungy, filthy with cobwebs, a strong rank smell of damp earth.

Yet she hears herself say in an earnest voice: "I—I think I will, thank you. Yes. I'd like to see what's in the boxes, that my husband left for me."

The Edricks have led her downstairs into the basement—as if she who'd lived in this house for twenty years needs anyone to show her the way. Here too, the widow feels both disoriented and comforted, for there are mismatched chairs and a plush dark-orange sofa facing an ugly TV screen that she has never seen before, yet the ceiling of loosely fitted squares is exactly as she remembers, and the olive-green floor tile is only slightly more worn.

Jed had detested TV. Their screen had been much smaller than this screen. She'd watched TV infrequently, always with a sense of guilt.

Your mind. Your brain. Beware of rot.

Mr. Edrick has dragged over a chair, that the widow might step on it to crawl through the waist high opening in the cement wall.

"Don't forget these! You will need both."

Almost gaily Mrs. Edrick presses a flashlight and a pair of shears into the widow's hand.

The widow steps onto the chair. The Edricks steady her, as she positions a knee so that she can crawl forward into a kind of tunnel like an animal's burrow, no more than three feet in height. A repairman might make his way into such a space on his haunches but the widow finds it easier to crawl—like an animal, or a child.

Her heart is pounding rapidly. Her nostrils pinch against the damp rank earthen odor.

The cramped tunnel is less than a few yards long. Yet, by the time she reaches the space itself, she is feeling light-headed from having held her breath for so long.

Why are you here? You are not wanted here.

Rats are more faithful than you have been.

With difficulty the widow lowers herself into the storage space. It is the size of a small bathroom or a large closet, with a puddled floor of broken cement; the feeble light of the flashlight reveals that there is an unexpected light hanging from the low ceiling, which she turns on—this too is feeble, no more than a forty-watt bulb. There are just two squat, badly water-stained and intricately taped cardboard boxes on the floor. The smell here is very strong, oppressive. Cobwebs stick to the widow's face, hair. If only she'd known to wear something on her head! And her open-toed summer shoes are not appropriate for this treacherous place. She hears a sound of scuttling—beetles. . . .

She is breathing very quickly now, near-panting. It is very difficult to get enough oxygen into her lungs.

The beetles have frightened her. Or, disgusted her. But she will persevere.

Such a low ceiling! This is indeed oppressive. She isn't able to stand upright but must crouch like a simian.

She tugs at one of the boxes, which is so heavy she can't budge it. Books inside? Jed had owned so many books, some of them oversized, first editions of mathematical classics. . . .

She couldn't possibly drag either of these boxes with her back along the tunnel. If she wants to bring their contents with her she will have to open the boxes and unpack them in the crawl space.

After much struggle with the shears, which isn't as sharp as she might have hoped, she manage to open the first box: indeed it is just books.

Of not much interest, she thinks. Disappointing!

Why had Jed hidden away *A History of Mathematics*, *Discrete Mathematics*, *A History of Zero*, *A History of Calculus*, *Infinity and Beyond*. . . . She'd hoped there might be something valuable here, and revealing; something Jed had not wanted to share with his wife, perhaps.

You don't want to know. Why do you want to know.

Suddenly she feels panic. A constriction of the chest, a wave of fear. Must escape!

She stumbles to the tunnel. She forces herself into it, crawling on hands and knees but what is this?—the way is *blocked?*

It must be a mistake of course. She has just crawled along the tunnel and knows that the way is not blocked, though it is disconcertingly narrow at one point.

"H-Hello? Mrs. Edrick? Are you there?"

No answer. She tries to force herself past the blockage, which seems to be solid rock, but she is frightened of getting just her head and shoulders through the opening, and being then trapped in this terrible place.

"Hello? What have you done? Help me. . . ."

No answer. She is trying not to become hysterical.

"Hello? Hello? *Hello?* What have you done? Mrs. Edrick? Hel-lo . . ."

No answer. No sound except her panicked breathing.

The new owners so resent her haunting the house, their property. They can think of no other way to stop her. Is this possible?

Of course, this is not possible. Ridiculous!

Yet they have gone away, upstairs. They have switched off the basement lights and they have shut the basement door. They will go away and leave their trapped visitor. They have planned this for years and when they return, the widow's cries will have grown faint.

When they return a second time, and a third time, her plaintive cries will have ceased.

Still, she calls for help. She thinks—*They are warning me, maybe. It is punishment for me—a warning.*

"Hello? Help? Mrs. Edrick! Mr. Edrick! I—I won't come back—I won't 'haunt' you . . . I promise."

She is begging. She is desperate. But there is no answer. They have gone away, they have shut the door at the top of the basement stairs.

No one's fault but your own. What did you think you were doing, joining me in the grave? Seven years too late.

Oxygen is fading. Her brain is fading. To occupy her mind, to occupy her panicked fingers she unpacks the first box fully—yes, these are all mathematical books, badly waterstained.

In some, Jed had made numerous annotations. What had the deluded man thought, that such fussy notes, such calculations, would make a difference?

The second box is more promising. Amid crumpled and stained sheets of newspaper used as padding there is something small, desiccated— mummified? A doll?

Not a human infant, the widow is sure. But disconcertingly lifelike.

Or—is it a human infant, so mummified that it has lost its human face?

Her hands are trembling with dread, and with excitement.

Cautiously she lifts the thing from the cardboard box, shaking off the stained newspapers. All about her is a scuttling of glinting beetles of which she is scarcely aware. She stares at the badly water-stained, faded face, a miniature face, with sightless eyes, broken glass, or plastic, or something that has atrophied and is no longer recognizable as even intended to be human.

The miniature pug nose has been mashed flat, the nostrils are smudged holes.

The mouth, a battered O like the mouth of a small fish.

"Oh! Poor thing . . ."

A wave of sorrow sweeps over her, the futility of all things human and nonhuman. She holds the doll to her chest, in cradled arms. She rocks it in her arms. Her eyes fill with tears, her pain is more exquisite than she could have guessed. So many years, so many days, yet no time has passed.

HEARTBREAK
1.

In the top drawer of my step-dad's bureau the gun was kept. It was kept unloaded.

They were laughing at the rear of the house. My sister Caitlin with her laughter like shattering glass and my cousin Hunt Lesinger who'd brought his .22 rifle over at Caitlin's request.

Giving her lessons in shooting a rifle. But not me, not even looking at *me*.

Showing off for Caitlin, is how it was. And Caitlin showing off for him.

In the mirror above the bureau—a flushed blurred face. I had learned to look quickly away from that face for so often I hated what I saw.

Mr. Lesinger's (forbidden) gun in my hand! Heavier than you'd expect.

(My stepdad didn't like it when I called him "Mr. Lesinger"—that did sound weird. He wanted Caitlin and me to call him "Dad." He put pressure on us to call him "Dad." But that was the name of our actual dad so how could there be *two Dads?* There could not.)

They were down by the ravine. I hated it, they'd gone off without me another time.

Behind Mr. Lesinger's house was an acre-sized lawn like a field that descended to a ravine, and beyond the ravine was Mineral Lake that was shallow and weedy at this end so you couldn't swim and even young kids wouldn't want to wade out in the muck on a hot day.

In the ravine was a wrecked car all overgrown with weeds and vines. Years ago someone had crashed his car through the guard railing up on the Herrontown Road, on a rainy night. The driver and his passenger had both died in the accident, in the ravine in what was called a "fireball" when the gas tank exploded.

This had happened long ago before we'd moved into Mr. Lesinger's big shingleboard house on Herrontown Road. Before Mom had married Mr. Lesinger and brought us to our *new life*.

Mr. Lesinger hadn't told us about the ravine or the car. It wouldn't have crossed his mind probably. Adults don't think of the most obvious things like what's behind your own house, in a ravine. Part of Mr. Lesinger's property was marshy and you wouldn't want to walk there.

The ravine was about twenty feet deep, and part of it was filled with trash. You could hardly make out the wrecked car covered with vines and badly burned, that looked like the skeleton of a giant insect.

Hunt Lesinger, who was Mr. Lesinger's nephew, knew about the wreck of course and the first time he came to visit us, after we'd moved into his uncle's house, he told us to come with him, he'd show us something we maybe didn't know about. It was a surprise to see the wreck back there, hidden from sight unless you knew what to look for.

First, we peered down at the wreck from the top of the ravine which was dense with underbrush. Then, Hunt wanted to climb down. He'd brought his .22-caliber rifle which he left on the ground for it was dangerous (he said) to climb anywhere with a rifle.

Caitlin hadn't wanted to climb down into the ravine—of course. But I was eager to follow Hunt.

Our step-cousin was the kind of boy you wanted to impress, by keeping up with him. Whatever he was doing. And if Hunt made jokes, you'd want to laugh.

It was awkward pushing through the underbrush then slip-sliding down the rocky hill, into the ravine. I'm a strong girl and my legs are hard with muscle but it was not easy going. A flurry of mosquitoes buzzed around my eager damp face.

Caitlin cried, "Wait for me!"

Caitlin was wearing flip-flops on her skinny white feet, short shorts and a tanktop. Caitlin was so *girly,* you wanted to laugh. You wanted to give her a swift hard slap to make her stop acting so silly.

"You never saw this? My uncle never told you?"

Hunt recounted how he'd been in sixth grade

when the car had plowed through the guard railing and it was in the local paper and on TV. His uncle had said how he and his wife had just gone to bed at about 11 p.m. and they'd heard the car hit the guard railing, then the crash in the ravine, without knowing what they were hearing, and then the terrible loud explosion when the gas tank blew up—"Like the end of the world."

Of course, both the bodies had been removed. There was no trace of anything human in the wreck (that I could see) that had turned black in the fire. All the windows were broken but little slivers of scorched glass remained in the frames like teeth. If you tried to climb inside the wreck, you could cut yourself pretty bad.

I thought of climbing into the front, behind the melted-looking steering wheel and the black-burnt dashboard, to sit on what was left of the seat and pretend to be driving, but decided against it when Hunt shook his head *No.*

"Better not, Steff. You could hurt yourself."

Caitlin wouldn't come too near the wreck—her flip-flops were so flimsy on her feet, she couldn't risk climbing down into the ravine. Saying in her throaty little-girl voice (the way she never talked around the house but only if there was someone special to impress) she was afraid of seeing something "awful"—(like bloodstains? parts of bodies?)—how terrible it must have been, those poor people skidding in their car on the road, and crashing through the guard railing—"They must have been screaming all the way down."

Hunt said they didn't have much time to be afraid, the gas tank had exploded within seconds.

Hunt laughed, the way a guy will laugh when he knows he has said something disturbing. There are some thoughts that scare you so, you have to laugh.

Caitlin put her hands over her ears as if this kind of talk upset her delicate nerves. "Oh Hunt, *please*. I don't like to think about it."

It was like that with my sister. The least thing she could turn to her own advantage, to draw attention to herself, she would. But Hunt could see through her, I think. He'd just laughed, as he and I were climbing out of the ravine, and didn't even answer her.

Later he said to me, "Maybe don't tell my uncle or your mom we were climbing in the ravine, O.K.? Just, they don't need to know."

It was thrilling to me, that Hunt would say this to me, in a quiet voice like we would share a secret.

2.

His name was Hunter—everybody called him Hunt. It was a nice name that suited him. And he was an actual *hunter*, too.

He was my cousin—I guess you'd say *step-*

cousin. First time we met, introduced by my mother, I knew Hunt and I would be in each other's lives forever.

"Steff, this is Hunt. You know—your new cousin . . ."

"Hi, Steff! Good to meet you."

Hunt was smiling at me, and it was a sincere smile. Hunt was not laughing at me. His eyes didn't slide away like guys' eyes do when they see, seeing you, that there's nothing to hold their interest but they need to appear polite.

Just then, Caitlin came downstairs. Even before Mom introduced them I saw how Hunt's eyes slid on my sister with her red-lipstick mouth and platinum-blond hair streaked with just-visible strands of purple and green.

In that instant, when Hunt lifted his eyes to Caitlin, I could see how he was forgetting all about me.

I hated Mom calling me *Steff* instead of *Stephanie* which is a much more beautiful name.

Steff makes you think of *Stuff*.

I think it is a deliberate thing they do, my mother and my sister, and everybody else, to put me down. Not *Stephanie* but *Steff*.

But when Hunt said "Steff"—it didn't sound so awful.

Hunt and his father Davis Lesinger had driven from Keene, New York, in the Adirondacks in his father's Jeep, to Morgantown, Pennsylvania, which is six miles south of Erie in the western part of the state. It was a twelve-hour trip they took once a year at least. The Lesingers were all hunters and Hunt and his father had brought two hunting rifles with them.

Hunt was proud to show us his rifle which was a Remington .22-caliber with a handsome polished stock—he brought it with him everywhere he could, he said.

Hunt's rifle was a registered hunting rifle. It was a legal gun in every way. When I saw Hunt lift it and squint through the scope I felt a chill along my spine but it was a pleasurable chill, of excitement.

Right away Caitlin said, "I want a shooting lesson! Ple-*ease*."

Hunt looked at Caitlin, and Hunt looked at me. It was like he was about to wink—at me.

Isn't your sister silly? How can you all stand her?

"Well, see—a rifle has a kick, Caitlin. It can hurt your shoulder if you don't handle it right. And the shot is loud."

It was startling to hear—how Hunt spoke the name *Caitlin*. So that it sounded special.

In this way, Hunt put my sister off. But knowing Caitlin, how stubborn and persistent she was to get her way, I knew this would be just temporary.

Hunt's mother was no longer in their family, it seemed. Hunt did not explain where she had gone and we would not have wished to ask our step-father Martin Lesinger who disliked personal questions especially from Caitlin and me.

"Maybe he's just like us, Steff! Except his mom left, not his dad."

Every summer Hunt and his father made the long drive from Keene to visit relatives in Morgantown. They stayed with his father's elderly parents for a week or ten days. It was strange for us—(Mom, Caitlin, me)—to think that they'd been coming to Morgantown all these years but we'd had no idea they existed.

Now that our mother had married Martin Lesinger, who was Hunt's father's younger brother, we were Hunt's relatives, too.

It was a surprise to Caitlin, and to me. I mean, a nice surprise. We had a brother Kyle who didn't live with us. (Kyle lived with our father.) But no other close relatives in Morgantown, or anywhere. No cousins our age. Suddenly there was Hunt Lesinger in our house and my mother laughing at the looks in our faces—"Girls, this is your *step-cousin*. Hunter is *family*."

Whatever else was said at that time passed by me in a roar. Must've been blood beating in my ears.

Seeing Hunt for the first time, and seeing how Hunt smiled at me, it was like something turned in my heart. Like one of those tiny keys you can hardly grasp with your fingers but when you do, unlocking a lock, a little door comes open.

I had never seen any boy that age, or younger, or older, as polite and well mannered as Hunt Lesinger. Mom had told us he was eighteen years old—he'd graduated from high school three weeks before. In the fall he had a scholarship to study forestry at the state college at Syracuse. He was a tall, lanky, long-limbed boy with chestnut-colored hair and a habit of whistling under his breath. He laughed a lot, but not loud or rudely. His favorite things to do (he said) were hunting, hiking, canoeing and camping in the Adirondacks. He hoped to work for the Adirondack National Park Service after he graduated from forestry college. In the fall he planned to enlist in the New York State National Guard.

Mom kept saying how cool it was, she had a "nephew" now—a "*step*-nephew." When she'd married Martin Lesinger eighteen months before she'd been hurt that almost no one from the Lesinger family had come to the wedding though most of them lived right here in Morgantown.

Mom's new husband was eleven years older than Mom. He had been Mom's boss at the Buick dealership where she'd worked until they were married, and you could see that he was still Mom's boss—the way he spoke to her, not exactly giving orders, never forgetting to say *Please* but in a tone of voice that meant there was no negotiating.

Of course, Martin Lesinger had been married before. His wife had died of some wasting disease like Parkinson's—there were pictures of her in the house, which Mom intended to hide away as soon as she dared. But Mr. Lesinger's children were all grown up and none of them lived in Morgantown, or had troubled to come to the wedding. Caitlin and I felt funny thinking how we had *step-sisters* and a *step-brother* old enough almost to be our parents whom we had never seen. That was weird.

Mom told us these *step-siblings* were "not overjoyed" about her marrying Mr. Lesinger whose wife had died just three or four years ago.

We asked Mom if these *step-siblings* were worried about Mr. Lesinger leaving money to her and not to them?—and Mom said she didn't think so, or anyway they shouldn't worry since she'd signed a *prenup*.

What's a *prenup,* I asked, and Caitlin turned to me with a sneer: " 'Prenuptial,' Steff. Everybody knows what a 'prenuptial' is."

The way Caitlin said *Steff* made me want to slap her. Like my name wasn't a serious name and could be shortened to some ugly syllable while her name was such a special name, she would not allow anyone to shorten it to *Cate*.

Mom explained to me what a *prenuptial* was. kind of legal contract Mr. Lesinger had asked her to sign, to acknowledge that she would receive

94

a "fixed sum" in the event of his death, and would be allowed to continue to live in Mr. Lesinger's house though she would not be the legal owner of the house, while the estate would be divided among the Lesinger heirs.

This did not sound right to me. Caitlin said she'd rather die than sign any contract like that—"If a man loved you, he wouldn't ask you to sign."

Mom's face reddened as if she'd been slapped. She told Caitlin she was speaking in ignorance. "There are different kinds of love. One day you'll find out."

But Caitlin just laughed and walked away, as if Mom was the most pitiful case she'd ever seen.

Did I hate my sister Caitlin? No.

Did I want to hurt my sister Caitlin? No!

3.

Mostly this was a happy time for our mother, after a long unhappy time. It was a happy time for Caitlin and me, too—at least, it was meant to be.

We lived in a bigger house now, on three acres of land edging Mineral Lake. We had a *step*-father now, not just a *father who'd abandoned us*. (As Mom used to tell anyone who'd listen.) Instead of a *dumped wife* Mom had become a *new wife*.

Mom was proud of her new name—*Mrs. Martin*

Lesinger. In the kitchen I found a piece of paper with *Mrs. Deborah Lesinger* and *Mrs. Martin Lesinger* written on it a half dozen times in red ink, that I ripped up and threw away. Embarrassing!

Caitlin and I still had our old name, which was our father's name—*Doherty.* When he'd had a few beers Mr. Lesinger spoke of adopting us which made Caitlin laugh, and made me want to run away and hide.

Caitlin was sixteen. I was thirteen. *Too damn old to be adopted.*

Anyway, could a man adopt another man's kids? Was that legal? Even if Dad had left us and moved a thousand miles away (as Mom was always accusing) he was still our father, and *Doherty* was our name.

It was just after my eleventh birthday that Dad left. Later he said he'd waited until then on purpose, so as not to spoil my birthday on March 5. (But every March 5 after that would be poisoned by the memory. Funny Dad hadn't thought of *that.*)

Dad told us he'd left not because he'd stopped loving us—that is, Caitlin and me—but because *Your mother and I no longer make each other happy.*

That is a scary thing, I think. As soon as you fail to *make a person happy,* they can leave you.

We knew that Mom and Dad had been arguing a lot but we had not taken it too seriously. For a long time they'd been arguing about the least little thing you could imagine like who had gotten gas for the car last or who'd left the thermostat too high. Or, when Dad spilled something in the refrigerator, he'd called for Mom to come clean it up, without giving a thought to cleaning it himself.

Near as Caitlin and I could figure our parents never argued about anything real at all.

Of course, we didn't know what they argued about when they were alone in their bedroom at the rear of the house. When they shut the door to that room with them inside.

In a family, one day is not so different from any other. Especially when you are very young—a "child." The important thing in life is routine. You can depend upon routine. There is comfort in routine. There is even comfort in the boredom of routine, for where there is boredom there cannot be fear.

Then one day, when Mom was at work, and Caitlin and Kyle and I were at school, something happened that had not ever happened before: Dad came back to the house in our absence, methodically packed his things into suitcases, backpacks, and boxes, and left.

Just left. Like that. And never came back.

It was hard to forgive Dad for telling Kyle beforehand. So Kyle was not so stunned. But Caitlin and me, and of course Mom, were really stunned.

Some shocks, you never get over.

Each morning when you wake up there is a sliver of time before you remember what it was that has happened, that cut your life in two so you have thought *I will never be happy again.* So for that instant you can be happy. But then your memory sweeps over you like dirty water and of course you remember what it is, or was—what it was that had happened, that cut your life in two and can't be changed.

Dad moving out was like that. When we came home and he was gone it was like some kind of scene in a movie, where people are made to look like fools for being so taken by surprise. Being shocked, starting to cry—an audience will laugh at you for being so clueless.

Afterward I could not remember how we learned where Dad had gone. Maybe Kyle told us. Or, Kyle told Mom. I think it was that—Kyle took Mom out onto the porch to tell her. Must've been something like *Dad is gone and says he isn't coming back. He says not to try to get in contact with him.*

Kyle was such a jerk, we could not ever forgive him. To keep from crying he kept making stupid jokes.

Of course we could see that Dad's things were gone. He'd swept his clothes out of the closets—his big jackets, in the front hall closet—so roughly, other things had fallen to the floor which he hadn't taken time to hang back up, or hadn't noticed. Not until the next morning did he call Mom, by which time Mom was in a very bad state.

It would turn out that in an argument Mom had told Dad—"If you're so damned unhappy all the time, just move out. We won't miss you!"

Mom had said such things in the past. Mom had sometimes screamed such things in the past. But Dad hadn't seemed to take it seriously, he'd just say something harsh and hurtful in reply, and it was soon forgotten, like water rushing along a riverbank. Except this time Dad had decided not to forget.

"Your mother told me to move out," Dad would tell us, with a smirk. "—and so I did. Hope she's happy now."

Saying such things meant that Dad wanted Caitlin and me to take his side against Mom. And maybe we did, sometimes. But we had to live with Mom and not with Dad, who didn't have room in his life for us (he said) but who'd agreed to take Kyle (there were special circumstances with Kyle).

Mom would say, in disgust—*Your father has abandoned us.* She'd say *Your father is a rat abandoning a sinking ship.* But she'd try to laugh to show that this was a joke, sort of.

Hearing that the family would be "split" I seemed to see something like a great tree that has been split down its center with an ax.

For a long time Mom refused to speak of Dad at all. If she had to refer to Dad she would say *your father*. If she was speaking to someone else she would say *The girls' father*. (As if Kyle, who wasn't living with us then, did not exist.) Mom's lips twisted like there was a bad taste in her mouth, or she was trying hard not to cry.

In this way our lives that had seemed so familiar and so routine became strange and shaken-up and complicated like a snarled ball of yarn. When Dad first left there were four of us left behind— Kyle, Caitlin, Mom, and me. Dad was supposed to see Kyle, Caitlin, and me on weekends except Dad's life was "difficult to schedule" and often he had to cancel; sometimes, he just didn't show up. Much of the time we had no idea where he was living, whether he was living alone or with someone. At one point he'd moved so far away, to Port Oriskany in New York State, it was a round-trip of two hundred miles, so coming to see us, to pick us up to take us to a movie and supper, was a hassle and Dad tended to blame us for it. Mom was having issues with Kyle "acting out" (Mom's term) so she and Dad decided that Kyle should live with Dad, at least temporarily, so Kyle went to live with Dad in Port Oriskany and started school there but then Dad moved again, back to Pennsylvania, to Jamestown which was closer to Morgantown at least. By this time Kyle was out of school but living at home and trying to get work. And then Dad got "remarried."

This was a real shock to Mom. Such a shock, you could surmise that Mom had (secretly) been hoping that Dad would return to her.

Poor Mom! Caitlin and I were ashamed for her then.

It sometimes happened, that people who'd been divorced would reconcile, and "remarry." It was a TV kind of happy ending. Though it happened so rarely you could almost say that it never happened, yet you wanted it to happen, you wanted to believe it might happen to you and your family.

Did I believe, sort of? Maybe.

But seeing how pathetic Mom was, I wouldn't have ever told her.

I was twelve years old and a tall "husky" girl for my age—almost as tall as Caitlin. I hid away to cry—I was ashamed of being so weak. I hated it when Caitlin cried which was mostly to get her way, not out of actual sorrow or grief but to make people feel sorry for her and do favors for her.

When Mom cried it was angry crying. Tears spilled down her cheeks that looked scalding. You had to run away!

It was around this time that Caitlin bleached her hair, and put purple and green streaks in it. Caitlin got her ears pierced, and a silver piercing in her nose, and started wearing the kind of sexy clothes Dad wouldn't have allowed her. (Dad was always saying he knew what guys are thinking when they see a girl dressed in a provocative way—"And it ain't nice. Take my word.") Caitlin became pushy and snotty and took out her bed temper on *me*.

Used to be, we'd been friends. Now, we were barely sisters.

Like Kyle I had "issues" at school so they sent me to the school psychologist who kept pretending to be sympathetic with me, encouraged me to cry if I needed to cry, pushed a box of Kleenex at me, and tried to get me to admit that I "hated" my parents for breaking up our home; I had to hate my mother for sending my father away, and I had to hate my father for leaving. But none of this was true. The only person I hated was the psychologist.

I did not hate my parents at all. I felt sorry for Mom, and all I wanted was for Dad to come back, we would all forgive him.

Then one day some older kids were pushing me in the cafeteria line, and I pushed back, and a kind of flame ran through me—*I hate you. Hate hatehate you.*

Seeing the look in my face and feeling how strong I was, so suddenly, they were frightened of me. They backed off fast.

From then onward, I did not cry. Not even when I was alone in my bed. After a while Dad became someone I saw at a distance, his face was small and blurred and no longer had the power to make me cry like a pathetic little baby.

Mom had a new better-paying job at the Buick dealership out on the highway. She began to take care with her hair and makeup and she dressed stylishly as she had not troubled to dress in years. She was often excited and distracted when she came home from work, late; many nights she *went out for drinks* with her friends.

Some of these friends were men, and sometimes these friends stayed overnight at our house.

Caitlin said it was "gross"—but better than Mom depressed and drinking alone. "Then we'd have to take care of *her*."

Mom began to go away weekends—Philadelphia, Atlantic City, Miami, New York City. Once, Las Vegas. Her friends were divorced men with children, in complicated relationships. Over a weekend there might be strangers for supper, and/or strangers who were house guests; kids our age, or younger or older, who used our bathrooms, slept on our living room sofa or in sleeping bags on the floor, asked if they could use our computer. Mom was always chiding *Don't be selfish, girls—this is my chance at happiness. There's plenty of room for guests here.*

One Thanksgiving there were eleven of us crammed around the dinner table. Don't even ask me who they all were. In the high-decibel noise even Caitlin was kind of silenced. It was like a tornado had rushed through the world uprooting houses and throwing people together who didn't belong together and did not even know one another but it seemed imperative that they sit together at the same table and *break bread together* as Mom called it.

Which was why I'd promised myself *Never me. Never get married and never any kids for me.*

Then, that phase ended. For Mom was seeing Martin Lesinger "seriously," and Mr. Lesinger was her boss at work.

Caitlin whispered to me, "Ohh gosh! He's so damn *old*" but I thought it was maybe a good thing that Mom's new man friend was older than Dad which might mean that he wouldn't get restless and leave her the way Dad did. He'd be *old,* and more settled in one place.

And this turned out to be so.

4.

"Hi, Steff."

Hunt saw me wince, and understood that that name was hurtful to my ears. So he began to call me "Stephanie" which no one but some of my teachers called me, and my heart melted.

When I was alone I said the name "Hunt" aloud. I did not dare say "Hunt" when another person could hear including my *step-cousin.*

While Mr. Lesinger and his brother Davis from

Keene, New York, sat together in the living room smoking and drinking beer and talking in lowered voices, Caitlin and I spent time with Hunt outside on the redwood deck.

It was a warm summer day and Hunt and Caitlin were in shorts but I was wearing my worn old jeans, to hide my thick thighs.

Mom says that I am *not fat,* just *big-boned.* Mom doesn't have a clue.

Caitlin and Hunt did most of the talking. Half the time it seemed like they'd both forgotten I was there.

It was like Mom to fret over the simplest things. You could see that Mr. Lesinger and his brother had a lot to talk about, in private, for a while at least, and didn't want Mom hovering over them offering drinks and things to eat. And every few minutes Mom would come outside laughing and breathless to see how we were.

"What can I get you, Hunt? Another beer?"

"No ma'am. I'm fine."

"I'm thinking of making some cheese puffs. Y'know what cheese puffs are? Think you'd like some?"

In her whiny voice Caitlin intervened: "Mom, Hunt isn't hungry. He just had lunch. We're going target shooting in the ravine, he's going to give me lessons."

"No. I don't think so. That is not a good idea. Martin would not like it."

Mom spoke vaguely, not really listening to herself. All the while she chattered at us she was attuned to the men in the living room as if fearing they might be talking about her. Or worse, not talking about her at all.

In the bright sunshine Caitlin's platinum-blond hair gleamed. Except for the purple and green streaks her hair was smooth and fine, and you had to concede that Caitlin was very good-looking, in a prissy spoiled way that I hated. For around Caitlin, everything had to be focused on *her*.

My hair was darker, a kind of muddy color. It was slightly coarse, not smooth, and my skin was slightly mottled, as if someone had rubbed it with a soiled eraser. It made me sick with resentment how Caitlin ate as much as I did, or almost, and was so sexy-skinny, while I was what Mom called *big-boned*.

Mom was always trying to make me feel better about myself. Using psychology, I guess. *Steff your eyes are beautiful. Thick lashes like that, I wish I had. . . .*

It was just bullshit. All I could do not to run away and hide.

Dad hadn't owned any guns but all the men in the Lesinger family owned guns. They were a hunting family, which was common in our rural county in western Pennsylvania, as it was common in upstate New York. Their favorite game was deer, which they talked about hunting, a lot.

I didn't like to think that my cousin Hunt who was such a kind person, and so sensitive, could bring himself to actually shoot a deer! I could believe this of the other Lesingers, and of most men in fact, but not of Hunt.

Martin Lesinger owned not only a deer rifle but a double-barreled shotgun which he kept "under lock and key" in the basement of his house; and he owned a handgun, a revolver, which he told us was licensed for "homeowner's protection." This revolver he'd showed Mom, Caitlin, and me just once, to warn us never to touch it.

But then he added, "Unless there's an emergency situation. Someone breaking into the house when I'm not here. Someone who has to be stopped."

Mom laughed nervously at this remark. Mom said she hoped such an emergency situation would never come up since she had no idea how to shoot a gun and would be scared to death to touch his gun. And Mr. Lesinger said, with a smile, the way you forgive a silly person whom you love, "All you'd need to do is shoot at the ceiling, Debbie. Or at the floor. Any intruder would get the hell out of here, seeing you with a gun." Mr. Lesinger laughed as if that was a comical thought, and Caitlin and I laughed too.

This gun, which was a ".45-caliber semi-automatic," as Mr. Lesinger described, he kept in a table beside his bed, unloaded.

Hearing this Caitlin dared to ask what good would an *unloaded* gun be? If you needed a gun for an emergency, you'd need it loaded. Like, if Mom had to shoot at the ceiling.

It was like Caitlin to pipe up with some skeptical remark. I saw how Mr. Lesinger stared at her as if he'd have liked to slap her. I didn't understand why he was so annoyed by her for asking this question which seemed like a sensible question which I'd have asked myself except I was too shy around Mom's frowning new husband unless maybe there was something we didn't understand. *Because the gun is not unloaded, see? Of course, the gun is loaded.*

This was complicated. Mr. Lesinger wanted us to stay away from his gun or—we had permission to use his gun? The gun was unloaded or—the gun was loaded?

Even Caitlin backed off asking more questions. Mom was smiling at all of us, obviously confused and waiting for the scene to be over—in her new marriage there were lots of scenes, like TV scenes, you found yourself in but mostly just waiting for them to get over. And Mr. Lesinger made me nervous when there was an edge to his voice.

When a man is irritated, it's like he might flail out with his fists. Not hard, and not to hurt, not even on purpose, but he just might do it, reflexively, and you might get hurt if you are standing too close.

And if a man hurts you, and you show that hurt, and your eyes lock with his, he will never forgive you. For always you will be the girl he *has hurt,* which means you are the girl he *can always hurt again.*

Mr. Lesinger put the handgun away in the drawer of the table by his side of the bed, shut the door firmly and said, "There!"

We were not sure what *There!* meant. But the scene was over.

In Mr. Lesinger's house on the first floor and in the basement TV room there were mounted deer heads. These were "bucks" as Mr. Lesinger explained. It seemed like more, but there were just three.

The smallest "buck" looked very young, and his antlers were not nearly so large as the other bucks'. Caitlin murmured to me *Oh gosh. I feel sorry for the deer.*

I felt sorry for the deer, too. It made me sick to think of anyone shooting such beautiful animals. Why didn't the damn Lesingers shoot themselves?—except for Hunt, I mean.

When we'd first moved into Mr. Lesinger's house we felt spooked by the mounted heads. Peering up at the deer's eyes you would swear were actual eyes, and not glass. And a deer's soul inside, peering right back out at you.

I am not so different from you. Why did you kill me?

I didn't kill you. It was a hunter.

But why?

I don't know why. I guess—hunters hunt. They like to kill.

5.

That afternoon, Hunt came to our house with his .22 rifle for target practice. Also, stolen away from a family barbecue at his grandparents' house, two six-packs of beer, a giant bag of tortilla chips, and some grilled (but still blood-leaking) hamburgers in soft doughy buns.

"Oh Hunt! What'd you *do!*"—Caitlin was thrilled.

They laughed together like young kids. Hunt looked at Caitlin the way I'd dream a boy might look at me—not just smiling and friendly but seriously *looking*. Like there was something in Caitlin's face that seemed to trap him, he could not look away.

Caitlin was wearing short shorts and a pink tank top, and her midriff was showing, and part of her flat little belly. It was disgusting to see her so damned smug about herself.

I'd tried to wear a tank top last summer but Caitlin told me it was embarrassing, I was just too fat. Mom scolded her for using the word *fat* but to me she said, "Caitlin is rude, but she has a point. You don't have the figure yet for that kind of clothing, Steffi." Trying to placate me by saying *Steffi,* not *Steff.*

Trying too to be hopeful suggesting that one day, not too far in the future, it might be suitable for me to wear the kind of tight skimpy clothes my sister wears. If I was lucky.

We were alone at Mr. Lesinger's house—Hunt, Caitlin, *Steffi.* The adults (including Mom) were across town at Hunt's grandparents' house where there was a family barbecue in the back yard. Caitlin and I been invited, sort of, but in such a way Mom had suggested we not come. Poor Mom had no choice but to accompany her husband and hope that someone in his family would take pity on her and talk to her about some other subject than how they missed Martin's deceased wife Evvie.

Hunt had only lingered at the barbecue for a while before driving to our house in his dad's Jeep as (I guess) he'd planned with Caitlin. It wasn't clear if his dad knew he was coming over to our house or if anyone knew.

Later, the Lesingers would express total surprise and shock that Hunt hadn't been at the family barbecue. They'd seen the boy, they would claim.

No one had seen him slip away, and back the Jeep out of the drive.

Caitlin put the hamburgers in the refrigerator for the time being. Hunt opened beers for all three of us but I couldn't swallow more than a small mouthful, the taste was so strong, and so bitter. When I started choking, Caitlin and Hunt laughed at me.

"Steff's way too young for beer, Hunt. She's 'underage.' "

"Yeh? What about you?"

"Not me. I'm just the right 'age.' "

They laughed together, excluding me. I was starting to hate both of them so hard it hurt.

Hating is hurtful. In the region of the chest.

Dressed like she was, and in flip-flops, Caitlin looked like some sort of silly sex doll. You could see the tops of her small white breasts and something of her skinny white back and her wrists were so skinny they looked like you could snap them like a twig. And laughing in that way that sounded like shattering glass, to rivet Hunt's attention. I'd never seen Caitlin *perform* so even on those nights Dad took us out to supper and we were thinking (maybe) if we could win Dad over, he'd come back home.

We were out on the redwood deck just hanging out. I had the thought that Caitlin and Hunt wanted to be alone but Hunt, at least, was too polite to say so. In his backpack he'd also brought a video—some episodes of *Game of Thrones* which Mr. Lesinger forbade us to see on his TV. Caitlin was saying we could watch it later, after target practice. While it was still light, she wanted Hunt to give her a lesson.

It was so, my sister was good-looking. Tl wild streaks of color in her hair, and her shii eyes, you could see why a boy like Hunt wo look at her like he did.

The thought came to me—*Maybe he will sh her. Maybe the gun will go off wrong. That shut her damn mouth.*

Oh but I didn't mean this! I was shocked think it.

Just a crazy thought that came into my head li some kind of vapor and evaporated almost once. It was hardly articulated in words. It was r a thought that belonged to *me*.

Hunt opened another beer for himself. Caitl was gamely trying to finish hers. We were eatir tortilla chips and Caitlin changed her mind abou the hamburgers—"Maybe we're hungry now. She looked at me like I should know how to reac to this remark.

I said that I would heat the hamburgers in the microwave. There was some ketchup in the refrigerator, I could bring outside. I was eager to volunteer to be useful—I liked to be helpful when I could be. As if I wanted people to like me, even if I did not like them; as if I wanted them to think that I liked them. Or maybe—*maybe I did like them, and badly wanted them to like me.*

So I went into the kitchen and microwaved the hamburgers for one minute—found the ketchup in the refrigerator and some cans of Coke; some

pickles, relish; leftover potato salad Mom had made the day before—and all this I brought outside on a tray, with paper plates and napkins, and salt and pepper in little crystal shakers that'd been filled (I seemed to know) by the woman who'd been Mrs. Lesinger before Mom. And when I pushed open the screen door—awkwardly, hoping I would not drop the tray—(Hunt and Caitlin would really laugh at me then)—and stepped onto the redwood deck—I was shocked to see that there was no one there.

I was just so surprised, I guess my mouth hung open.

"Hi? Hello . . . ?"

I had to suppose they'd gone down by the lake, or by the ravine—(where else could they get to, so fast?)—but there was no one in sight. It was weird, maybe it was comical—I set the tray down on the picnic table, walked from one end of the redwood deck to the other, looking for Caitlin and Hunt—calling, "Hi? Hey? Where are you?"— kind of pathetically saying, "Your hamburgers are ready. . . ."

It occurred to me that they'd hidden around the side of the house. In the garage? In the TV room in the basement?

All that I knew was, they hadn't come into the house through the kitchen. At least I knew that.

Steff! You're looking kind of lost.

This was so exactly what my mother would have

said, I almost seemed to hear it. Mom's voice close in my ear.

But Mom wasn't there, no one was there. No one had spoken.

Where Caitlin and Hunt had got to—I just couldn't figure. If they'd gone back to the ravine, that was kind of a long walk for them to get there so quickly, unless they'd run. (But why would they run? Why would they run away from *me?*)

Looking kind of lost. That was a sad thing for Mom to say, but it was true. Mom was always scolding me for being not "well groomed" like Caitlin—(she'd say *other girls your age* but I knew she meant Caitlin)—but I guess deep down she loved me, and felt sorry for me. But when people are nice to me that's when I cry, and feel really bad. And so I said, "I hate them both. I wish Caitlin would fucking *die*."

This was shocking to Mom and me both. This was the first time I had ever said such a thing even to myself.

Mom looked at me in amazement. *Watch that mouth of yours, girl.*

I turned away so that Mom could not see. My mouth was working but no sounds came out.

You know, we don't allow the f-word in this house. That's crude and vulgar and your sister knows better too and if your step-father heard he would be disgusted. And if anybody hears, they will think you are lowlife. You should be ashamed.

Some minutes then I called—"Caitlin? Hunt?"
—I trotted all the way to the edge of the lake,
where the soil was marshy and kind of smelly, and
over to the ravine, where tall weeds and saplings
were so thick you could barely see the wreck
below—I could see that they weren't in these
places but still I called, "Caitlin? Hunt?" like a
fool. If this was TV people would be laughing at
me. An invisible audience would be laughing at
the fat girl *looking lost*.

I returned to the redwood deck, and around the
side of the house to the driveway—there was
Hunt's dad's Jeep, that had not been moved.

(I'd had the sudden fear that they'd driven
away in the Jeep, and left me. Maybe they'd
decided to go to the Lesinger barbecue but had
somehow forgotten *me*.)

But then, I went into the house. It had not
occurred to me that they might have entered the
house by the front door, and might be somewhere
inside the house.

But they were nowhere in the first-floor rooms.
No one here except the mounted deer looking
at me pityingly. *Lost girl. Lost like us. Trophies on
the wall. Pathetic.*

I was sweating now, and breathing quickly. I
was feeling so ashamed!

I stopped calling "Hunt?"—"Caitlin?"—
reasoning that if they didn't hear me call them,
they couldn't be blamed for not answering me;

but if I continued to call them, and it was clear that they heard me, it would also be clear that they'd played a trick and hidden from me, and that would be mortifying.

I went back out onto the redwood deck, and they still were not there. A fly was crawling over one of the hamburger buns but I was too distracted to chase it away.

Caitlin's beer bottle had been set down on the picnic table. I think the bottle had to be Caitlin's, it was just half-full.

There were at least two empties on the table. These had to be Hunt's. (But had he had a third, in his hand? Had he walked away with this bottle?) The bottle from which I'd taken just a sip or two was where I'd left it on the flat railing top.

I snatched this up and took another swallow. So bitter! But I managed to keep it down, out of spite.

They'd gone somewhere, and Hunt had taken his beer bottle with him. Maybe. (I saw now, Hunt's rifle was lying on the deck, where he'd placed it. And his backpack. These had not been moved.)

I wondered if I should wait for them to come back? Obviously they had not gone far.

Obviously, it was some sort of joke. On me.

Not a mean joke, just a joke.

"Yo, Steff! Hiya."

Suddenly there came Hunt's laughing voice—and Caitlin's high-pitched laughter.

They'd been downstairs in the TV room, after all. There was an entrance to the basement around the side of the house which I guess I'd forgotten. I stood there on the deck blinking and confused but after a minute, I was relieved to hear myself laughing.

Laughing so hard it hurt my belly. For I'd managed to finish the bottle of beer, and I was feeling—well, weird.

What do they call it—*buzzed*.

Hunt and Caitlin were telling me—(like they expected me to believe this!)—that they'd decided to experiment with the TV, or the DVD player, just to see if it was operating. "For later, when we watch the video." Hunt was carrying a beer bottle, in fact. His smile was lopsided and boyish and his words were slurred.

"Like, we might want to stream a movie. If the DVD doesn't work out."

Why was Hunt telling me so much? Like it seemed important to him, that I would believe him.

I opened another beer for myself with the bottle opener. The little cap went scuttling across the flood of the redwood deck and we laughed, seeing this.

We sat at the picnic table and ate the food I'd set out. Caitlin wasn't very hungry for the lukewarm hamburger—"Damn, Steff, this is hard as a rock! What'd you do to it?"—but she drank the Coke thirstily. Hunt devoured two hamburgers soaked with ketchup and more than half the potato salad. "Thanks, Steff! This is great."

Steff. He hadn't even noticed what he had said, that he'd picked up from my sister.

Caitlin said that meat was *gross.* Eating animal muscle and tissue was *gross.* She'd been thinking, maybe she would become a vegan.

"Meat is protein," Hunt said. "Vegans get skinny and sick."

"Caitlin is skinny already," I pointed out.

It was an inane remark but everyone laughed including Caitlin.

Then, Caitlin said, "Steff, is there ice cream? In the freezer?"

"No. I don't think so."

"Maybe—go look?"

There wasn't any ice cream in the freezer. Mr. Lesinger had a weakness for ice cream so he forbade Mom to buy it. Sometimes we were allowed to have frozen yogurt, but there wasn't any frozen yogurt in the freezer, either. Caitlin might not have known this or was pretending not to know.

It was a signal for me, to go into the kitchen and check. To bring a container of ice cream out onto the deck, and three spoons.

So I went inside, but had to use the bathroom. And when I came out of the bathroom I checked the freezer that was crammed with packages of meat and leftovers but no ice cream.

I found some ginger snaps in the cupboard. On a high shelf, where Mr. Lesinger asked Mom to put them, so he couldn't reach them easily, or he'd finish the entire box. These, I brought outside.

This time, as soon as I stepped out onto the deck, I saw the two of them walking away—not hurrying, and not glancing back—toward the ravine.

"Hey? Hunt? Caitlin . . ."

Hunt was carrying his rifle slung over his shoulder. Caitlin had talked him into giving her shooting lessons. If Mom knew, she'd have been upset. Mr. Lesinger wouldn't have liked it, either. The mean thought came to me—*Caitlin will get in trouble now. They both will.*

On the deck I stood watching them, thinking my thoughts. The beer helped me think more clearly. *I am not going to chase after you again.*

Instead, I cleared the picnic table. Like I didn't give a damn about them, or had even noticed them. Damn buzzing flies! Ketchup-soaked napkins, Caitlin's shredded hamburger and bun. Smeared mayonnaise from the potato salad on all the plates. And the empty beer bottles, and tortilla chips crushed underfoot.

I hate you so. Hate hatehate you so, wish you were both dead.

I thought that I would behave responsibly, as Mom might do in such a situation. When Dad had said awful things to her, and made her cry, she'd retreat to the kitchen to clear away dishes, to clean up. Sometimes she'd scour the stained linoleum, squatting on her haunches on the floor.

We avoided Mom at such times. Caitlin, Kyle, Steffi.

Poor Mom! She's pathetic.

Just stay out of her way.

Inside the kitchen I could watch them from a window. They were at the ravine now, just standing there. I tried to imagine what they were saying to each other but I could not. Without me, they would talk of things I could not imagine. This was so painful to me, I was drinking a second, maybe a third bottle of beer. The buzzing at the back of my head was louder now, and exuded a yellow light. Almost, I could see that light if I shut my eyes.

I heard a shot—had to be Hunt with his rifle.

Desperately I thought—*I am not chasing after you. Not ever again.*

Upstairs in the big bedroom where Mom and Mr. Lesinger slept, on Mr. Lesinger's side of the bed was the table, and inside the drawer was the gun.

Never touch. Except emergency.

I saw myself opening the drawer, and I saw my hand lift the gun out—it was *heavy*.

Really, I was just watching. The buzzing at the back of my head had spread to the front part by my eyes and I was watching what I did through this buzz, that was like fluorescent lighting.

The gun in my hand, *.45-caliber semi-automatic*. There was something scary about it but comforting as well. Like, something so heavy in your hand, and your hand was given a certain distinction.

If this was TV, or a movie close-up. The girl's hand, and the girl herself, at which you wouldn't wish to glance for more than a second, given a certain distinction.

I did not think—*Is the gun loaded?* For some reason that thought did not occur to me at all, as I had not (somehow) thought that my sister and my cousin might've hidden from me in the basement TV room, when the door was right there around the corner.

Some things, you just don't think. Though later you would realize these were the first things that you should have thought.

It seemed to take a long time to hike to the end of the field, that prissy Mr. Lesinger liked to call a lawn. The sun was hotter than before and my eyes were beginning to get blurry.

Hunt and Caitlin weren't at the ravine now but over by the lake standing in the marsh where cattails grew to the height of a man's shoulders. There was trash here too, that had spilled over from the ravine in a heavy rainstorm. Hunt was sighting along the barrel of his rifle, aiming at something in the lake—a glittering patch of water. He fired, and Caitlin gave a little squeal of fright. But it was insincere fright you could see.

Caitlin wasn't eager now to take the rifle, I guess. She'd liked flirting with Hunt but when it came to actually taking the rifle from him, she wasn't so sure.

I called out to them, "Hey! Hi! Look what I have!"

Hunter turned, and when he saw the gun in my hand he didn't seem so welcoming as I had imagined. And Caitlin was looking shocked.

I'd thought my cousin who loved guns would be impressed by this gun. I'd thought for sure he would be impressed with *me.*

"Steff, for God's sake! What is that—a gun?"

Caitlin was shocked but also disgusted. She didn't seem to notice my flushed face, that felt hot and swollen. The buzzing in my ears was like a roar.

"Is that—*his gun?* You took out of his bedroom? Oh my God."

Hunt was trying to smile at me, but I could see that Hunt was also disapproving.

"Is that my uncle's gun, Steffi? Maybe you should put it down."

I told Hunt that I wanted a gun lesson, too. I wanted to learn, too.

Caitlin said, "That is not a plaything. That is Mr. Lesinger's gun. You put that right back where you found it. We won't tell anyone but you'd better do that—now."

I knew my sister would say this. Or something

like this. It was like Caitlin to spoil anything I wanted to do, when I was poised to be happy for once.

I did not mean to do anything but scare Caitlin. She was so mean to me, and seemed to be ashamed of me. The mistake was, I know that it was my mistake but it was also Caitlin's mistake, that she was so nasty to me. She was sneering, and stuck-up, and full of herself, and she didn't give a damn about me. When we were with Dad, she got all the attention from him. Like all the light in the room, or all the oxygen in the room, and didn't care about me, and how lonely I was.

So disgusted looking at me as if she shouldn't have been scared of me. Respectful of me.

For I had Mr. Lesinger's gun, which I had to hold in both hands because it was heavy. And I was pretending that it was loaded. I was pretending that it would really shoot if I pulled the trigger. "Get down! Get down on the ground, you are arrested!" I was mimicking cops on TV programs, like *Cops*, that's what the cops always shout at the pathetic whiskery drunk men they're trying to arrest. *Get down! Get down on the ground!* The men are slow to obey sometimes out of defiance but sometimes because they are dazed and drunk and disbelieving. Sometimes they are even half-naked—bare-chested, and barefoot. Ridges of fat at their waists spilling over their belts. You see them on TV and feel revulsion for them, which is a disgusted kind of pity. *What do his children think! Does he have a daughter? How can she show her face at school? She is more shameful than I would ever be.*

Caitlin was saying mean, sharp things to me. Caitlin was threatening me she'd tell Mom and Mr. Lesinger about me. Caitlin was sneering like she didn't even know me, I was so far beneath her. Caitlin came forward to slap at me, or to take the gun from me—that is what I remember.

And the gun going off—that is what I remember.

How I was ducking away in the marshy grass, and the mud was sucking at my feet. And the gun must have shifted in my hand. The direction of the barrel shifted. In that moment I seemed to have no control over it, the gun was too heavy, it is not like the idea of a gun that is exciting but the actual weight and feel of a gun, that is something differ-ent. For maybe Caitlin did not rush at me and try to slap me, but I would remember the look in her face of disgust. And Hunt looking kind of sur-prised and scared and he's saying *Stephanie hey—don't aim that at us.*

Hunt was reaching toward me, and Hunt had pushed Caitlin back, behind him. As if to shield her. Shield her from *what!* I was furious seeing this, because there seemed to be a misunderstanding. And it seemed that I would be blamed. I shut my eyes. I did not pull the trigger but— the gun went off.

There was a loud *crack!* Mr. Lesinger's gun went off by itself and jerked from my hands and fell into the mud.

I knew then, something terrible had happened. It wasn't my fault, it wasn't Hunt's fault. If there was any fault it was Caitlin's but Caitlin would not be the one who was punished.

Saw Hunt on his knees in the marsh grass, and that look of shock and hurt and fear in his face. And blood like a burst dark flower on his T-shirt, high on his chest. And Caitlin screaming. And my screaming, too—I think it was me screaming.

6.

"Stephanie?"—the voice is firm but kindly.

In this place there is an air of acceptance, unsurprise.

There is not what you'd call trust, exactly. I see in their faces, in their eyes, that they are not comfortable with me, or with other court-mandated juveniles who are like me, though they may feel kindly toward us, and they are accepting of us as *outpatients* receiving court-mandated therapy. We are *work* to them, and they are *working* to make us well.

I have not told any of the staff at the clinic, I am sick with heartbreak. I have told them that I am very sorry for what I did though with a part of my mind—(it is possible that the more experienced

126

among the staff can "read" this part of my mind but I pretend that I don't know this)—I don't truly think that what happened was my fault, or my fault entirely. *My sister! My sister is to blame.*

Hunt did not die. But Hunt took a long time to recover, after emergency cardiovascular surgery to save his life.

Hunt would not be enlisting in the New York State National Guard, or in any of the armed services. Hunt would probably not be strong enough to hike, hunt, camp in the mountains as he'd loved to do.

I would not ever see Hunt again. I knew this.

Soon after the "gun accident"—(as it was called)—I was sent away to live with my father and his new wife in Jamestown, Pennsylvania.

Partly this was because Mr. Lesinger did not want me in his house any longer, ever again. But also, Caitlin had come to truly hate me. (She had not hated me before, I realize now.) And Mom seemed fearful of me though she insisted that she was not and that she loved me *just as much as ever.*

It was thought best that I go away to live somewhere else where (mostly) no one knew me. A new home, a new school district. In the Morgantown family court it was decided that as a first-time juvenile offender I would receive *psychotherapy* and *counseling* as an outpatient. I would not be *incarcerated* in any facility.

Dad has full-time custody of me now though I think he is not so happy with this arrangement, and I know that his wife is not at all happy. And even Kyle is fearful of me, at times.

For I have become one of those persons of whom others will say—*There is something not-right about her. Be careful of her.*

Even if they don't know who I am, and what I did, or caused to happen, in a "gun accident" when I was thirteen years old. Even if they don't know that I am sick with heartbreak they will say of me—*That one, Stephanie. Just be careful around her.*

It is really true, something is wrong with my heart. I can't breathe deeply the way I once did, my chest hurts. I can't sleep more than an hour or so at a time—something just wakes me up, like a slap. I hear a girl's sharp scolding voice—I hear a girl screaming. And I sit up in bed, gasping for breath. In the dark I am anxious of what the day will bring. Sometimes I see a dark ravine with something glittering deep inside it. There is a lake, and there is no opposite shore that I can see, but it is known to me that if I can swim to that shore, I will be all right again and my cousin Hunt will love me again.

In this place, I am so lonely. But I am lonely in all places for I carry my loneliness around with me like a heavy backpack.

No one calls me *Steff, Steffi* any longer.

THE DROWNED GIRL
1.

It was a 1,500-gallon rooftop water tank in which she died.

Her naked body so decomposed, after eleven days, that water from the tank was badly contaminated—teeming with the bacteria of decay, rot.

Yet for eleven days this water was piped into the building below, a shabby three-story brownstone on Pitcairn Avenue called *The Magellan* in which students who could not afford residence halls on campus rented "off-campus" rooms.

Most were foreign students. Graduate students.

A few were undergraduates, technically—but not full-time, and older.

Turned on the faucet in my bathroom and water sputtered and gushed and it was discolored, foul-colored—feculent-smelling.

Before this for maybe a week it was just the water pressure was low. You'd turn on the faucet and a little trickle would come out. But it had not seemed discolored then. Or, in the dim light, I could not see clearly.

Appalled, nauseated, I let the water run—gush and splash—must have thought that it would "clear up"—would become drinkable!

For some reason I turned on the shower also. Just to see—if—though I must have known better—the water spraying out of the shower-head was discolored also. Of course, it was.

" 'Miri Krim.' "

Often, I whispered her name aloud. Shut my eyes to see a butterfly's shining wings—"Miri."

But "Krim" was a sharp deep cut. Razor cut, so quick blood doesn't appear immediately and when it does, you're shocked to find blood on your hands.

She was nineteen when she'd died. Drowned.

That's to say, *was drowned.*

For certainly Miri Krim had not drowned accidentally. Not in such a terrible place, and in such circumstances!—and not *naked.*

Nor had she (as some [male authorities] tried stupidly to argue) killed herself.

We (girls, women) know how we would kill ourselves, if/when we undertake to do so. And we know—*it would not be in a rooftop water tank. And it would not be naked.*

I did not live in *The Magellan*. But the fascination of *The Magellan* drew me.

Each day I passed the building on my way to the University campus. First, I passed by the side of the building that overlooked Humboldt Street;

then, I turned left, and passed by the front of the building, that faced Pitcairn Avenue.

You could not see the water tank from the street. No.

It was *her building*. Though Miri Krim was dead, and no one had ever convincingly explained how she'd died, and newer tenants in *The Magellan* pretended not to know her name, the building was yet *hers*.

Mir-i Kim? Never heard of her I'm afraid.
Who? No.
What's the name? Chinese?
Sorry. Maybe someone else can help you.
Nooo.

In high school I'd become interested in epidemics. Infectious diseases. In *Scientific American* I'd read a terrifying matter-of-fact article on Ebola— the twenty-first-century "scourge."

Our school library in Adirondack, New York, was very limited. Our computers were old, malfunctioning. Yet, I managed to write an ambitious term paper on rabies for my Biology and Ecology course, which my teacher praised to our class, and for which he gave me a grade of A+.

(Invisible) (teeming) pathogens burrowing into the (helpless) body, bent upon the destruction of the (unwitting) host—this was fascinating, awful.

I did not believe in God. But I had always taken

131

comfort in the God-belief of adults. But now it seemed to me (obvious) that these others did not believe either. No one could seriously "believe" that God cared for man any more than God cared for the pathogens He had created with the power to annihilate mankind utterly.

Drowned girl. Water tank. Rooftop.
  Girl-body to which (unnamed) things were done.
  Had I known of Miri Krim before enrolling at the University? I think that I did, yes. I did know. Something.

That is, I had *heard*. At our community college. But I did not truly *know*.

Such an atrocity is like a shadow, or an eclipse. You "see" it with your eyes but you cannot comprehend its meaning. Nor can others explain when it is so very ugly.

It is not often possible for me to access a computer at the University library. The computers there are always in use. On the screen of my battered laptop is a permanent message—*You are not connected to the Internet.*

Is this in mockery? Because I am a transfer student from upstate, and an "older" student? Because I am not one of the "affluent" students at the University?

At the housing office they are not so nice, if you are "older"—a "part-time" student. If you depend upon student loans and "deferred" tuition.

Not that they sneer at you openly but there is a look of coldness.

I am several years older than Miri Krim would be if Miri Krim were still alive. I am a first-year student at the University, in the School of General Studies, in which Miri Krim was a second-year student.

Though I am a transfer from Adirondack Community College the University did not accept the three courses I'd taken there, in which I had earned all A's. And so, unjustly in my opinion, I am but a first-year student at the University, at the age of twenty-five. And I am not (yet) allowed to take the courses I want to take.

In the School of General Studies there are not *freshman, sophomores, juniors, seniors.* We are not so coddled for we are part-time students, and we arc (usually) older than undergraduates.

We do not pay the tuition paid by full-time undergraduates. We pay by "course credit"—like counting pennies into the damp smelly palm of a stranger's hand. However many pennies it is not ever cnough.

I am not bitter. I am not a bitter person by nature. Bitterness does not "run in the family"— that would not be a Christian way of behavior. Many times I have expressed my gratitude at being allowed to enroll at the University under the *deferred tuition payment plan* that is available for students who have met certain requirements.

After her death it would be revealed that Miri Krim was *in debt* to the University. Just $1,700 which does not seem like a great sum except if $1,700 is, to you, as it is to some of us, a great sum.

Accounts of Miri Krim's death were carried by national news services for a day or two and then vanished. Locally, in Hudson County, which is where the University is located, further information was provided, or perhaps leaked, that Miri Krim was *in debt* to the University and that, at the time of her disappearance, her attendance at her classes was *erratic.*

Sometimes it would be primly noted that Miri Krim was *a transfer student from an upstate community college.*

(Miri Krim had attended a single semester at Allegheny County Community College which is several hundred miles south and west of Adirondack Community College.)

(Miri Krim and I did not know each other. Only inhabitants of downstate New York could think that upstate Allegheny and Adirondack are anywhere near each other.)

(Not only had we never met but the possibility of such a meeting is virtually nil since we did not attend the University at the same time.)

(What does "nil" mean?—*a nothing beyond Nothing.*)

• • •

But for *The Magellan*, would Miri Krim be alive today?

In the foyer by the mailboxes we'd see her. We thought.

Turned out, maybe that wasn't her—the one we were remembering.

Miri Krim moved into *The Magellan* on September 6, 2010, and on April 30, 2011, she was reported to have "gone missing"—though her absence was not much noted on that date since she had few friends and attended classes "erratically." Neighbors in *The Magellan* did not (usually) see her every day.

As days passed, Miri Krim's absence became more evident.

In *The Magellan* Miri Krim lived (alone) in 2D, a second-floor room with a single window overlooking Humboldt Street.

The Magellan is not University-owned but it is University-approved.

The Krims are bringing a lawsuit against both *The Magellan* and the University for "criminal negligence" in their daughter's death.

On the morning of May 10 Miri Krim's lifeless naked badly decomposed body was discovered by a building custodian floating, faceup, in the water tank on the roof, in eleven feet of water. By this time water in *The Magellan* was clearly contaminated. Discolored water gushed from every faucet and showerhead. Tenants complained of a *God-awful taste, nasty smell*. Police officers who'd previously searched the building, including the roof, were summoned to return, to accompany the custodian to the roof another time.

That water tank? Let's take a look.

Two men required to lift the heavy cover.

It was disgusting! It was so, so terrible. . . .

To think that we'd been drinking that water— cooking with that water—until it became so discolored, you knew something was wrong.

Jesus! I knew. I think I knew. Like, right away. Something was wrong. Maybe I thought it was rust in the water like from the pipes.

You figure, brushing your teeth—that doesn't require much water, mostly toothpaste. . . .

When I arrived at the University in September 2011 people were still talking about *the drowned girl, the girl in the water tank*. But it was rare for anyone to speak the name *Miri Krim*.

The Hudson County coroner's report had not been released until August. Why the autopsy had taken so long was not explained.

Then, the result was inconclusive: *suicide or accidental drowning*.

Many were disbelieving, and angry. *How had the drowned girl managed to drown herself in the water tank? How had she gotten up on the roof, how had she lifted the heavy cover by herself?*

If there'd been injuries to Miri Krim's body, the body was too decomposed to identify these injuries. If Miri Krim had committed suicide, there was no note left behind.

If there were "suspects" who lived or worked in *The Magellan*, or close by, who might have had the opportunity to have abducted, raped, and murdered Miri Krim, no one of these was ever arrested.

There had been a rape kit and this rape kit was said (by the coroner's office) to have been "misplaced" (by the coroner's office).

Like gnats such thoughts pass through my head. Sometimes in my large lecture classes the low persistent buzzing is such that I can barely hear the professor's voice and I must stare and stare like a lip-reader.

It has come to be a habit of mine, a compulsion, to glance over my shoulder during the class, to (rapidly, unobtrusively) scan the faces of the strangers behind me, for it seems to me, as in one of those perception tests in which identical figures are repeated in rows and one, singular figure is hidden among them, that *the drowned girl* is among them.

Her face, a dead girl's face, among the faces of the living.

I try to brush these thoughts away usually without success.

Those moments when her presence is felt.

Even before I learned that Miri Krim had lived in the brownstone building I passed every day, and that her second-floor window overlooked Humboldt Street, often when I passed the side of the building my eyes lifted to the second floor, to a window there—*as if a figure in the window was beckoning to me.*

I did not see a face in the window but rather a rippling reflection of a (pale) face. If I paused to stare, the reflection dissolved.

Soon after, when I learned that the nineteen-year-old from upstate New York had had a room in that building, I understood (I think I understood) why my eyes lifted to one of the windows and it did not surprise me (it would not surprise me when eventually I learned) that this was in fact *the window of room 2D.*

If I had enrolled at the University a year earlier we might have seen each other: *Miri Krim* at the window as *AlidaLucash* (that is my name—I know, it is not a beautiful name) passed below on the sidewalk.

In that fleeting way we "see" others who are strangers to us with no thought of how we will enter into each other's life at a later time.

Often then, after I knew, I would linger at the front entrance of the building and I would peer into the foyer. If no one observed I would enter the building (for there was no lock on the outer door) and I would examine the mailboxes. But the mailbox for 2D has no name—not even a small rectangle of white upon which a name might be printed.

Excuse me! Are you looking for someone?—it might be asked of me. And I would say—*Miri Krim. Did you know her?* And the answer would be a pretense of ignorance, or outright denial— *"Kim"? Some kind of Korean name?*—and I would say *Miri "Krim," not "Kim." She used to live here* and the reply would be stiff and unfriendly: *Well, I just moved in.* Sorry.

After Miri Krim's partly decomposed body was discovered in the water tank *The Magellan* was immediately shut down by authorities and all tenants were relocated as a massive overhaul of the water pipes was required by the county board of health. Not surprisingly, few of these tenants wished to return to 803 Pitcairn and so it was possibly true, those who claimed not to have heard of Miri Krim might have been telling the truth.

Since September 5 of this year I have been living at 22 Humboldt Street in a private residence in which I rent a single room and share a bathroom with another tenant, a young woman of my approximate age. Our landlady is a retired University professor.

Humboldt Street is a street of (somewhat

139

run-down) frame Victorian houses that have been partitioned into rooms. Proper lives—family lives —were once lived in such houses. Verandas and front porches, the remains of carefully tended lawns.

In the weed-splotched back yard at 22 Humboldt, an aged, cracked clay birdbath containing what appeared to be the small skeleton of a bird but which turned out to be (when I inspected) some broken twigs.

It is a three-minute walk to *The Magellan* at the corner of Humboldt and Pitcairn Avenue, fronting Pitcairn.

Though there is a rear entrance to the apartment building. A narrow alley behind *The Magellan* where a Dumpster and trash cans are kept. A mild odor of rot prevails here.

From the sidewalk you cannot see the water tank on the roof of *The Magellan*. From room 2D you could (possibly) see the roof of the brownstone apartment building on the other side of the street, where there is said to be an identical, 1,500-gallon water tank.

In one of my courses the Professor inquired of the class how could we recognize the *front of an object?*

The question was put to us like a riddle which the Professor did not (evidently) expect anyone to answer.

I did not know the answer. I could not guess the answer.

I am uneasy with riddles. I feel always that someone is laughing at me and (indeed) there was a smirk on the Professor's face when finally no one in the class could think of an answer and so he said, "The front of an object is the side that provides the most information."

Is this so? I had never thought of such a thing before but it is true, the "front" of a living being tells you so much more about it than its rear or sides.

However, there is minimum of information provided by the weatherworn façade of *The Magellan*. An entrance, a portico, six steps, a heavy door. Three rows of windows.

Inscribed in a cornerstone, 1931.

Often I linger in front of *The Magellan*. As if I am waiting for someone to come out and greet me.

I have made a graph of my courses. Each assignment, each quiz, each test, each grade.

So far, my grades have not been as high as I have wished.

To retain my *tuition deferral status* I must maintain a grade-point average of B.

At the present time, my grade-point average is somewhere below B.

I am determined to excel. I will not be discouraged. Except it is distracting to me, when I try to read my textbook assignments and take notes strange thoughts flood my brain that don't belong to me but to another.

Went missing! As if I was not taken. As if I'd gone—willingly.

And my clothes torn from me. And what was done to me—ruled an "accident."

Such thoughts, inhabiting my brain. And the emotion borne with them, of hurt, anger. Fury.

But these thoughts have caused me to think: what does *went missing* mean?

As if you could *go missing*. Of your own volition.

As if *missing* were a place you could go to, and not a condition.

As if a *missing person* could be *missing* categorically. As if there is not (surely) someone who knows where she is (even if she does not know herself where she is).

Missing person—missing body.

Floating (naked) body of Miri Krim beneath a lid so heavy it required two men to lift it.

So beautiful—the face perfectly preserved, like a doll's face. Eyes open and unseeing.

And the hair (previously brown) faded to silvery white, and thinned, floating around her face like a halo when the men heaved the lid up and an overcast light fell upon her.

But the rest of her, submerged in water . . .

. . . bloated, putrescent. Unrecognizable.

Of course, Miri Krim had been raped. And worse.

Terrible things done to Miri Krim, that would never be named.

Why the coroner's office "misplaced" the rape kit.

Why the police have not arrested any "suspect."

Why no one wishes to speak of her any longer and it is fear of her death you smell on them.

2.

"My dear. Someone in this house is shamelessly *wasting water*. Candace has assured me, it is not her."

Our landlady Professor Ida Schrader regards me with reproach as soon as I enter the foyer of her house. But I am too quick for the frowning woman, already I am on the stairs and hurrying to the second floor, to my room.

Not me, either, ma'am—these words are flung over my shoulder almost giddily, defiantly.

And not a backward glance for I know very well how Professor Schrader is glaring at me through the thick lenses of her silly plastic glasses.

Wasting water. Shameless!

It is true, often I allow the water to run in the bathroom sink for some seconds. Maybe, a little longer.

Dreading to hear if the old pipes protest. If the

old woman downstairs whose hearing is not so sharp will hear the pipes and when she sees me next, berate me for *wasting water*.

Everywhere I am obliged to use a bathroom, a lavatory, a public restroom, I let the water run for as long as I dare.

Stooping to examine the water that gushes from the faucet.

Its transparency. Its smell.

The drowned girl took this route. This street, these steps.

It is her advice to me, to fear airborne infections. For airborne bacteria are invisible, undetectable, unavoidable.

Befouled water you can see, smell. Befouled air you can't see and by the time you smell it, it may be too late.

There is little choice, you have to *breathe*.

I am feeling her presence on Pitcairn Avenue. At the underpass beneath the New York Central railroad tracks, that is always dank, dripping.

Pavement always puddled, in the shapes of prone, sprawled figures. Shallow pools of stagnant water thick as pus.

Like me, Miri Krim took this route to the University—of course.

There is no other route from Pitcairn Avenue to College Avenue and the long hill to the Hall of Languages. No other choice.

Quick! Run.
Try not to breathe.
Try not to breathe deeply.

North of the underpass, College Avenue. Long sloping hill into the campus protected like a fortress by wrought-iron fences, gates.

It is difficult to gain access to the University campus if you come from College Avenue. There are gates, and there are security officers.

If you are "suspicious-looking"—(as most [white-skinned] students are not)—you must show your I.D. to a security officer at a kiosk.

Sometimes, though I am white-skinned, the officer frowns at my I.D. and insists upon inspecting my backpack, instructing me to empty it out entirely and yet he seems still about to shake his head *No*.

It is a relief to me then, my heart floods with gratitude, when the officer mutters *O.K.*

Wondering if Miri Krim had ever been rejected. If her skin had seemed, in a certain overcast light, a brown-tinctured skin, olive-dark, not "white."

But Miri Krim was a student, if but a student enrolled in the School of General Studies. She would have had a valid I.D., the security officer would have muttered *O.K.,* and gestured her through.

Hurrying up hill to the revered old Hall of

Languages (1849). Ponderous gray stone that looks damp like something hauled from the depths of the ocean.

The Hall of Languages bell tower is a famous bell tower illuminated by night and visible for miles like a moon.

You would be able to see the bell tower clock in the distance like a glowing moon if you stood on a rooftop on Pitcairn Avenue. From a second-floor window, or from the street, you could not see it.

But sometimes, in the stillness of the night, you can hear the bells tolling.

Invisible bells, and the sound of their tolling almost inaudible, vibrations you feel rather than hear, like the beating of a great heart.

It is strange: when I pause to listen to the bell tower, I am not ever able to determine what "time" it is.

In University brochures you do not see the urban neighborhood that surrounds the historic old campus. You do not see the dripping underpass, or Pitcairn Avenue—of course!

You see photographs of on-campus residences, and of the large, showy fraternity and sorority houses on the farther side of the campus, that is called Greek Hill, but you do not see pictures of off-campus residences.

You do not see pictures of *The Magellan*.

(Like me) Miri Krim was enrolled in the School of General Studies. It was her belief that she was enrolled in a *pre-med program* but so far as I have learned there is no *pre-med program* in the School of General Studies.

I had not thought of medical school. Everyone in my family would be astonished. Miri Krim is an inspiration to me.

My courses in the School of General Studies are introductory courses. Though my grades were A's at Adirondack Community College I am not (yet) allowed to take any course numbered beyond 100.

Would I be allowed to enter the pre-med program next year, if I do well in my courses?—I have asked the advisor assigned to me; and this kindly-seeming man told me, with a look of sympathy, or pity, for this may be a naïve question often asked by General Studies students, "Well, possibly. Yes. If you do well in your courses and can transfer out of General Studies and into Arts and Sciences."

If you do well. Can transfer.

This is reasonable, I thought. Of course my fate depends upon my academic performance.

Shyly then I asked, and daringly, in a rush of words: "And if I do well in pre-med, I will be accepted into the University Medical School?"—and my advisor said, with a little frown, "Why, yes. That is—possible."

The University includes a distinguished School of Medicine as well as distinguished Schools of Law, Finance, Engineering.

I did not dare to ask *Is there financial aid available for medical school?*—for my advisor had been glancing at his wristwatch and seemed uncomfortable. Clearly it was time for me to leave.

Other "older"—"part-time"—students like me were waiting in the corridor to see him. You signed up for an advisor, for ten-minute slots.

Yet at the door I paused and asked, "Did you know a student named Miri Krim, Professor?"

How strange, that I asked this question! I had not intended to.

Adding, seeing the man's quizzical look, "She was in this program too."

" 'Mu-ri Kim.' I don't think so."

" 'Miri Krim.' A friend of mine."

"No. Sorry"—(my advisor glanced at my name, on the manila file before him which he was about to put away), "—'Alida.' We have many advisees in the School of General Studies, you must know."

He did not type the name *Miri Krim* into his computer. How easily he might have done this. Yet he did not.

He knows that she is dead. That is why.

"Goodbye, Alida. Good luck with your courses."

My advisor spoke with a false sort of heartiness. And beneath, contempt and disdain that one as lowly as I would dare to speak of such matters.

A notation was made in my file, which I would never see.

• • •

They will hate you now. They will try to hurt you.

From that point, my experience at the University was poisoned.

No matter how hard I studied for any quiz or test, no matter how much I researched a paper (in the University library, not merely on the Internet like other undergraduates), no matter how carefully, how obsessively I worked—my grades were low, barely passing.

Errors were made in the bills sent to me. The interest rate on my student loan was raised without my knowledge. It was stunning news, that my debt to the University was $3,100—before I had completed even my first semester.

Thursday evenings, at the University Medical Clinic on Eleventh Street.

Lie on your side, dear. Make a fist.

Giving blood is not painful. As the needle enters a kind of anesthetic/amnesia floods over me: cool, antiseptic. It is a white noise of the soul, and it is comforting.

Sometimes at such moments I shut my eyes very tightly. The tolling of the hour, close by, yet sounding as if it were distant, muffled and fading, is calming to a quick-beating heart.

Payment is cash. Thank God, not a check!

We don't trust checks. A check can be *canceled*.

In time, I come to recognize some of the

regulars. Of course, we are not allowed to sell our blood too frequently, careful records are kept.

In a restroom stall hurriedly I count the bills. Shaky hands, one or two bills will flutter to the floor which is a filthy floor in rebuke of my greed.

Not so much cash as I'd hoped. Or maybe I'd misunderstood.

But it is something, and something is far better than nothing.

And it is *cash*.

South of the underpass. Pitcairn Avenue.

Once, the avenue might have been a busy street. But no longer.

Here are old brick and brownstone buildings grim as smudged erasures. Cracked pavement through which weeds poke like coarse lace. Stink of exhaust, diesel fuel. City buses groaning and heaving from curbs, spewing more exhaust. Off-campus student housing, married students' housing, International Students' Center, African-American Center, Hudson County Family Services. Old Victorian houses donated to the University for tax purposes. And close by, liquor stores, taverns, pawnshop and nail salon, Laundromat, Bethel Tabernacle Church, Rite Aid . . . *The Magellan*.

A "mixed" neighborhood where some people are friendly-seeming and others stare at me as if they'd like to grab my backpack and run away with it.

How many times Miri Krim must have left *The Magellan* to take the underpass to College Avenue, and to the University. And on these many occasions, all except one, nothing happened to harm her.

Had she been stalked? Had she been warned? Threatened?

Had she had a premonition? Had she suspected —something?

And so just once something happened to interrupt the routine of Miri Krim's life. Almost certainly it happened on the south side of the underpass. In *The Magellan*. And the young life of Miri Krim was extinguished as you might blow out a flame.

No arrests? Why are there no arrests?

Why is the murderer (or murderers) being shielded?

"*Not* a race thing. Not so simple."

It was Professor Ida Schrader, my landlady at 22 Humboldt Street, who insisted that the danger in the neighborhood had nothing to do with race but with drug dealing (which appeared to be "mixed-race") and with the "downward spiral" in the American economy that matched a "downward spiral" in the American soul.

Somehow, in Professor Schrader's mind, this

"downward spiral" was connected with global warming.

It wasn't clear if global warming had precipitated the decline of the economy, or if the decline of the economy had precipitated global warming.

"That girl, the one who was drowned and her body left in the water tank just up the street—she is exactly what I mean."

These harsh words Professor Schrader spoke disapprovingly, with a shudder of her large tremulous bosom. As if the *one who was drowned* had brought such a fate on herself, endangering the rest of us.

"Yes! Police said, she was involved with drugs. Probably she was high—or drunk—and went swimming in that water tank. Or, she committed suicide but the family paid to hush it up. Or"—Professor Schrader drew a deep breath of reproach—"one of her drug-addict friends murdered her, and now—we must live in the toxic fallout."

I did not like to hear such terrible words. Like poisoned toads hopping from the Professor's mouth. And Candace Durstt, the other tenant, did not object but seemed actually to agree, in her eagerness to curry favor with our landlady.

Females who should have been sympathetic with Miri Krim.

In Professor Schrader's house we did not often encounter one another. Perhaps we avoided one another. Yet sometimes in the first-floor corridor encountering one another could not be avoided.

On a table in the foyer Professor Schrader placed our mail in two distinct piles. Neither Candace Durstt nor I ever received much mail, and what we did receive was mostly advertising flyers, or notices from the University.

Professor Ida Schrader had lived in a high-gabled faded-peach-colored Victorian house at 22 Humboldt Street for nearly forty-seven years, she'd told us. The house had been a "family inheritance"—a "beautiful domicile, originally" —that had suffered in the "moral, cultural, and political collapse" of the late 1960s.

"You never know around here when you might be stabbed in the back or dragged off into an alley or your house broken into or torched. You can be wary and cautious—you can be a 'good girl'—but you will never know."

Seeing the look in my face Professor Schrader said quickly, "Oh, it isn't just colored people— 'persons of color'—who are hostile to us. I know this as a fact. It's our fellow 'whites' too, the ones on welfare and drugs. And 'hippies'—whatever they call themselves today. 'Street people.' "

Professor Schrader spoke vehemently, with an air of bitterness and chagrin. Yet, she was capable of reversing herself by seeming to laugh at her own words—"Oh, listen to *me*. Just an old white 'intellectual' fulminating, in an age of digital illiteracy."

Professor Schrader was a retired professor of anthropology, once chairman of her department. She was a heavy woman with wild white hair, pendulous breasts and upper arms, legs as thick (nearly) as my waist, and a squeezed-together, almost childlike face. She wore enormous billowing "slacks"—as she called them—with stretch waists and short-sleeved T-shirts for she perspired easily, even in cold weather. Her eyes were all but hidden behind the thick lenses of her plastic harlequin glasses yet you could sense their cunning and you could see in the set of her mouth a withheld smirk, a look of deep suspicion. Yet often, she seemed bemused by me—"My apparition"—(glancing at me over her bifocal lenses with a look of mock-fright). "Heavens! You are always sneaking up on me, Lide."

Her name for me was "Lide"—("lied"). Why this was amusing to her, I don't know.

"Candace" was "Can-dace" to her—sometimes "Can-*dance*." This too was amusing, to Professor Schrader.

I had had few conversations with Professor Schrader. She seemed to prefer a kind of banter as if I were one of her students, but not a prized student.

I did not know how to react to her remarks—

her witticisms. Was she being insulting, or teasing?—or friendly, in a bullying way?

On the subject of *the drowned girl* she was particularly vehement. It was clear that *the drowned girl* preyed on her mind a good deal.

I could not understand why Professor Schrader and now Candace Durstt were so unsympathetic with Miri Krim whose very name they seemed to have forgotten, as if she, and not her murderer or murderers, were a threat to them. Speaking of her with disdain as *the drowned girl* who deserved the terrible thing that had been done to her. (Though I was certain that neither Professor Schrader nor Candace knew the details of the death.)

At last I said: "Miri Krim was nineteen years old. She was a student at the University who was raped and drowned—murdered." My voice was shaking badly but I continued, as Professor Schrader and Candace Durstt stared at me in astonishment. "No one was ever arrested for the crime. The police didn't seem to have looked very hard for the murderer. Miri Krim was not a drug addict—that is just a rumor. She was an *honor student*."

Hurrying then to the stairs. Not a backward glance. For I knew the two were staring after me and I knew that, as soon as I shut the door to my room, the Professor would make an unkind, witty remark about "Lide"—"poor Lide"—

"lied"—and Candace would snort with laughter through her wide dark horse's nostrils.

It was not true, strictly speaking, that Miri Krim had been an honor student at the University. But Professor Schrader and Candace Durstt would not know this.

I had read (online) that Miri Krim had been an honors student at Allegheny Community College, and that she'd graduated salutatorian of her high school class. At the University, however, for reasons not known, Miri Krim had ceased attending classes in the last several weeks of her life.

Her first-year grades had been uneven— sprinkling of B's, C's. In chemistry, a forlorn D.

My grades, too, have been "uneven." But I am determined to excel.

My attendance record at the University is perfect. On my graph of all my courses, for each class day I have noted this. Usually I arrive early for lectures to sit in the front row. (It is not clear to me, however, if attendance is taken in University courses. For we do not have assigned seats as in high school. I do not want to think *Of course, nobody cares if you attend a lecture, or not. Why on earth would anyone care about you?*)

It is crucial to sit in the front row in lecture halls for at the University lecture halls are immense holding as many as three hundred students.

I am the girl who sits in the front row in Hall of Languages 101 directly in front of the podium. So that, if the Intro to Psychology lecturer (Professor Gee) happens to glance out into the audience, he will be likely to see me, and it is possible that he will wonder who I am, who is this girl so serious, so attentive, so concentrated upon note taking in a spiral notebook, amid rows of bored and distracted undergraduates with laptops opened before them, or cell phones semi-hidden in their hands.

Professor Gee may make inquiries. He may make a notation in his class file.

Lucash, Alida. Pre-med.

Passing *The Magellan* on Pitcairn, and around the corner on Humboldt Street. Resisting the impulse to glance up, to squint and smile at the face in the window that fades—(but not slowly: teasingly) even as I stop dead on the sidewalk like a figure caught in a rifle scope.

A faint, fading voice. *Alida! I am so lonely.*

A disturbing scene this evening at the University Medical Clinic.

An older student came to sell his blood, and was lying on a table near me, on his side, his eyes were tight-shut, and his hands were fists; but when the attendant came to him, it was with bad news—he was not to be allowed to give blood any longer, for he was HIV-positive.

(Did I overhear something I was not supposed to overhear? I shut my eyes tighter, and tried not to hear. For I *am not an eavesdropper* and I take no pleasure in the sorrows of others.)

He objected: "No. That's wrong. That's a mistake!"

Yet the young man was refused by the clinic. He was instructed to roll down his sleeve and depart. For he would not be allowed to sell his blood at the Medical Clinic, not ever again.

"You are fucking mistaken, *I am not HIV-positive.*"

A furious young man of my approximate age, though his hair was badly thinning and his hands shook. No one wanted to look at him—it was clear that this was a sick person, and that his blood was infectious and unwanted.

Such persons are infectious and unwanted. Their medical files are flagged.

He continued to speak loudly, threateningly. A security officer was called. His words were rapid and slurred. The irises of his eyes were dilated. The eyeballs of his eyes were jaundiced. I did not want to be seen observing him for I recognized the terror in his voice, and I knew that a terrified person can turn on you like a maddened dog as if you are an enemy and not a friend.

Out in the corridor, the young man began to cry.

"Please! You should help me—shouldn't you? Somebody has to help me."

Faintly we heard him as he was escorted away: "Please—I don't want to die. . . ."

It is surprising, the "hidden fees" in the University's monthly bills.

For instance, all enrolled students, even those who are part-time in the School of General Studies, are being charged a (new, unexpected) three-hundred-dollar "student center" fee. (There is a capital campaign, the University is hoping to raise one hundred million dollars for new development including a "palatial" student center.)

I can't pay this fee. I just can't. My expenses are budgeted and there is no extra three hundred dollars. . . .

Eventually, the fee will be added to my loan. With interest.

"I hate them. I don't trust them at all. Especially *her*."

It is Professor Ida Schrader whom I most distrust. I have reason to think that the Professor charges me more for my room each month than she charges Candace though Candace's room is larger than mine, and the ceiling appears to be higher than the ceiling in my room, and there is a far nicer view from her single window than there is from mine which looks out upon an alley resembling the College Avenue underpass.

In September, I might have moved into another University-approved rooming house, or into an apartment building (like *The Magellan*—but I did not know the history of *The Magellan* then)—except the rent in Professor Schrader's house was attractively low and "kitchen privileges" were included; plus, I would need to share a bathroom here with only one other tenant, another "female" like myself.

Online pictures of the high-gabled Victorian house at 22 Humboldt Street are very attractive, also. You could not see the peeling paint like decaying skin. You could not smell the bathroom drains, or the stark stale graveyard smell of the interior of the refrigerator.

Alida, take care. Do not trust them.

This faint, sweet voice I knew to be her voice. But I did not reply to her, just yet.

Often I am stricken with shyness, when a friend approaches. A new friend, the promise of a new friend, a new love—vertigo overcomes me.

They are not your friends. They do not wish you well.

If you could take my hand . . .

In the solace of sleep, sometimes. Warm fingers brushing mine beneath the bedclothes.

It is always a shock, bare feet on bare linoleum floor, a wailing sound in the water pipes when I dare to turn on a faucet. To avoid the others, I have begun to wake early, while it is still dark.

In the bathroom that is adjacent to my room and to Candace's room on the second floor of Professor Schrader's house, I take pains to wipe the toilet seat several times with toilet paper. (Such an old toilet seat—made of wood! A cheaper, white-plastic seat would be preferable, I am sure. Bacteria cling to a porous surface like wood, and breed in its microscopic cracks. Bacteria are exposed on the sleek surface of plastic, and more easily extinguished.)

Professor Schrader will complain of *water wasting* but I am obliged to run the water until it gushes steamy-hot from the faucet. I am obliged to use as much soap as necessary to clean the toilet seat and other areas of the bathroom. My dread of germs in communal places has grown in recent months, since my arrival at the University.

In my former life before the University, there did not seem to be a fear of contagion—there did not seem to be an awareness of the possibility of contagion in our small town in Adirondack County.

I do not like "sharing" space with the other tenant, or indeed with Professor Schrader. Sharing a bathroom with Candace Durstt is particularly unpleasant, for I do not like this young woman, and I do not trust her; I know that, with Professor Schrader, she laughs at me behind my back, and jeers at me, and (possibly) Professor Schrader gives her a key so that she can prowl in my room,

161

and go through my things; if she could, she would peer into my computer (as into my soul) and learn all my secrets, except that my computer is malfunctioning, and a rainbow icon spins obliviously, maddeningly, whenever you raise the screen.

Often, the screen to my laptop is black. Blank-black. The power cord malfunctions, too.

It is strange, though I dislike Candace Durstt, and shudder at having to touch the toilet flush handle, faucets, shower knobs, etcetera, which Candace also touches, I do not (truly) think that Candace is a bearer of lethal bacteria, as Professor Schrader may be; Candace Durstt exudes an air of dryness, not of moisture, in which bacteria thrive. But there is a particular unease in imagining the heavyset perspiring older woman lowering her buttocks onto the (cedar?) toilet seat. . . . It makes me feel faint to imagine those fleshy, pocked buttocks, a pale doughy flesh creased and cracked and *oozing*.

No! I do not want to envision such a sight.

Professor Schrader has her own bathroom of course, which is attached to her bedroom at the rear of the house, on the first floor. (Which I have never seen. I have no wish to see.) But she (sometimes) uses "our" bathroom, when it is convenient for her. (Professor Schrader has difficulty walking, and does not move about the interior of the house any more than is necessary.) Sometimes Professor Schrader murmurs an apology of some sort, which is hardly sincere, and horse-faced Candace will say, with a braying laugh—"Oh Professor, of course we don't mind! This is your house." (As if the bullying old woman needed to be reminded!)

Did I mention that Candace is an anthropology graduate student? She is tall and spindly-limbed like an arachnoid; you have to look twice at her, to see that she has only two arms and two legs. There is something cobwebby about her mouth, a trace of spittle in the corner of her lips. Truly, I try not to look.

Initially Candace had seemed (almost) friendly to me—she had come upon me looking very distressed (but not crying, I think), holding in my shaking hand a letter from home, one of my mother's misspelled and ungrammatical but razor-sharp letters; Candace had encouraged me to speak to her of the sorrow in my heart, that my parents had had a change of mind and wanted me to return home, that they had decided they could not "afford" me to be away from them, and to be "costing so much money"—(which was a cruel joke for they were not paying a penny toward my University expenses); I had confided in Candace, that the University was to be my "salvation"—(knowing even as I spoke that I might regret such extravagant words in which, to a degree, I did not actually believe; for I understand that, even with a University degree, and strong letters of recommendation from my professors, I will have a difficult time securing decent employment in this era of rampant unemployment). Another time, reeling from my first math quiz, in which I had received a grade of 17, Candace had insisted upon examining the sheet of paper crudely marked in red ink like slashes in flesh, to see if possibly there was some mistake; she'd been kind, assuring me that she had no aptitude for math at all, and admired me for daring to take such a course which was not, strictly speaking, a course usually taken by students in the School of General Studies.

Yet soon after this, seeing an advantage in aligning herself with our landlady against me, Candace turned disdainful and aloof to me, and will often stare bemusedly through me when, by chance, we happen to meet on campus.

In one of my University courses it has been suggested to us, in terms of scientific causation, with its (essentially) materialist foundation, that there is no *chance,* or *accident;* there is only *determinism, necessity.*

Of course, there is no *free will* in such circumstances. I did not want to raise my hand to ask the Professor—*Is everything decided, then? Why are we studying here? Why do you bother" to test us, when our grades are determined beforehand? And all of our lives?*

Here is another question: why have Professor Schrader and Candace Durstt bonded together, in their dislike of me?—I am trying to comprehend.

Is it because they are each quite unattractive, in very different ways? The one obese, and asymmetrical (the Professor limps, favoring a swollen right knee); the other tall and spidery-limbed. While Miri Krim was (judging from photographs) a very beautiful girl with classic features: wide-set eyes, a small straight nose, a small sweet mouth. Her hair seems to have been just slightly wavy, and wheat-colored; it fell to her shoulders, and she often wore it brushed behind her ears. Not carelessly, but casually. Her eyes were dark, and intelligent if just slightly dreamy.

Did she know? Did she foresee? Was it determined?—"fate"?

Did she go willingly with her abductor/murderer?—did she resist?

Was there no one to hear her cries, no one to save her? Was this determined, also?

The more you gaze into the eyes of *the drowned girl*, the more you peer into her soul. The experience is—well, it is very unsettling.

Before her death Miri Krim weighed (approximately) one hundred pounds; after her death her poor, ravaged remains weighed scarcely fifty pounds. Before her death, Miri Krim stood approximately five feet, one inch; after her death, her remains were so decomposed, they could not be helpfully measured.

Unlike Miri Krim I am not a beautiful girl—indeed. I know and accept this.

Yet, it is a coincidence that I appear to be approximately Miri Krim's size—my weight is one hundred six pounds, and I am five feet two inches tall.

Yes, *petite*. How I hate *petite!*

My hair is brown, a very ordinary color, and it is not wavy; my eyebrows and lashes are unusually pale, as if invisible; my mouth is small and unassertive and my smile (if I dare to smile, in the presence of Professor Gee, for instance) is a very shy smile.

It is easy for large persons to dismiss me. My professors at the University scarcely notice me at all.

Also, (large) persons like Professor Schrader and the sycophant Candace Durstt.

"It's an honor to be your tenant, Professor Schrader. I am so grateful!"—shamelessly Candace flatters our obese landlady.

Candace is always asking the Professor if she can borrow a book from one of the Professor's bookshelves, which are crammed with books on obscure subjects. (Professor Schrader has an impressive collection of books! But most of them are old, and quite a few appear to be waterstained and warped.) The Professor never fails to be flattered—though she sometimes pretends to be annoyed. "Yes. Of course, dear. If you promise to return the book to *exactly the same position you've taken it from.*"

As if she does not trust Candace, even while allowing herself to be flattered and manipulated by her, Professor Schrader records the title of the book to make sure that it is returned.

The Victorian house at 22 Humboldt Street appears large from the outside but inside, its rooms are surprisingly small and cramped. There are remote rooms which we rarely enter. Each of the rooms is lined with bookshelves and in one or two of these, out of playfulness (not malice) I have removed a book from a shelf and placed it elsewhere, on another shelf.

Has Professor Schrader noticed? I never check to see if the book has been returned to its original position for this would be a giveaway, if the Professor caught me.

Ida Schrader had been a renowned anthropologist, it seems. Until, in the 1990s, her field of aboriginal research had "collapsed." Charges were made against (white) (American) anthropologists that they were exploiting native subjects—"aborigines." Even worse, many anthropologists were accused of inventing data. In some cases renowned anthropologists were misled by their (canny, conniving) native subjects, who humored them as inquisitive fools or provided them with sham information, like counterspies. Such charges had been made against the most famous of American anthropologists, Margaret Mead, with whom Ida Schrader studied decades ago; so Ida Schrader felt herself hounded into early retire-ment, and ceased publishing. Her physical decrepitude made it unlikely that she could continue to travel to distant aboriginal fields of inquiry in such places as Australia and Papua New Guinea, in any case.

It is ever more fearful to me to enter the bathroom between Candace's and my rooms and to sniff the air cautiously—(against my will: *I do not want to be sniffing in such a place*)—to detect if Professor Schrader, with her particular odor, has used it in my absence. My cleaning and scouring rituals have become ever more intricate. Of course I bring my own towels into the bathroom for I do not trust the Professor or my fellow tenant not to use them. The face in the medicine cabinet mirror is wan, blurred; the eyes are bruised and wary. (Are these my eyes?) I have to suppress a sob for I feel keenly the futility of my efforts to avoid contagion, as *the drowned girl* similarly failed not only to avoid the contagion of death but becoming, herself, in her physical being, after her death, an object of contagion. *To become putrescent, to leak through plumbing and discolor water gushing from strangers' faucets, to arouse terror and disgust in these strangers*—it was a horrific fate for anyone but particularly for a beautiful young woman who had (surely) been conscientious in her grooming and cleanliness, and would have been stricken with shame if (for instance) she had smelled of her underarms in a public place, or appeared in public in soiled clothes.

A fate which (I told myself) I must avoid.

Though Candace Durstt left her toothbrush and toiletries in the bathroom, and sometimes even articles of underwear drying on a towel rack, like a shrike-bird who blatantly displays its prey, I took my toothbrush and toiletries, as well as my (damp) towels, back to my room. It was too great a risk, that one or both of the others might take my toothbrush and defile it in the toilet bowl; the mere thought made me nauseous. Sternly I told myself *But no one would do such a thing. Not even these people who hate me.*

Contaminated showerheads. Mold. You can become very sick from mold. Infectious spores. A kind of tuberculosis, a severe and chronic bronchitis. Your voice is faint, tentative. You are the bearer of a ferocious cough, that drives others from you in disgust.

The heat, the damp of a shower. Spores flourish, teem in such places. Colonies of mold spring into being, as much in the world as humankind. It is deflating to realize that you are not privileged over the mold in your showerhead.

In your lungs the spores breed wildly. Damp,

heat, dark, secrecy. You find yourself thinking one day as the mold bids you think. You wake—*But this is not the way I was yesterday. Something has changed.*

I had read of Legionnaires' disease. Waterborne mold spores, streaming over the face and body of an (unwitting) individual, a potentially deathly contagion.

Carefully I removed the showerhead in the bathroom, and replaced it with a shiny new showerhead purchased at the hardware store on Pitcairn at my own expense.

I told Professor Schrader that the old shower-head had fallen and cracked and that I had gone out at once to purchase a new one.

Professor Schrader was speechless at first. She heaved her bulky body up the stairs, panting, to examine my handiwork. How bright the new showerhead gleamed, like a stainless-steel moon! Clearly, this initiative on my part surprised Professor Ida Schrader and was forcing her to reconsider me.

At last she said, frowning: "All right. But I can't deduct the price of the showerhead from your rent. I hope you are not expecting that."

I had not even thought of that! (Well, perhaps I had thought of it: I had saved the receipt.)

"Because in fact you broke the old shower-ead, Alida. That was carelessness on your part."

Though it was not true, I could not deny this.

· · ·

(Yet soon, within a few weeks, the gleaming new showerhead lost its luster. The interior of the shower was perpetually humid. A smell of drains prevailed. On the showerhead, as on the faucets, a splatter of soap scum which I took pains to clean away, with steel wool if necessary.)

Here is a strangeness. I do not want to think what this strangeness means.

In one of the remote rooms in the Professor's house, on a shelf of antiquated-looking hardcover books, I have discovered a paperback chemistry textbook—so heavy in my hand, I can hardly hold it. On the inside front page of the textbook a name has been crossed out in black marker ink— a name that resembles, but may not be identical with, MIRI KRIM.

Quickly returning the heavy paperback to the shelf, before someone observes me.

(The possibility that Miri Krim rented a room here, before moving to *The Magellan*, is deeply disturbing. But I dare not ask Professor Schrader.)

Laundromat on Ninth Street. Has to be the Laundromat that Miri Krim used.

That smell of hot laundry, when you open the big tumbling drier.

Brushing a hand against another's. Eyes averted. But we are smiling, we recognize each other.

Ours is a bond of vengeance. We are waiting!

Yeah she came in here sometimes. Think it was her. That girl who drowned in the water tank . . .

Hell no, for sure she didn't drown herself. Somebody did that for her, that was never caught.

Had to be some guy works in the building. Or somebody connected with law enforcement, that there's a cover-up for.

Terrible! Like her spirit is here, with us.

We are all that is left of her. Us.

Eighteenth-century University buildings. Gabled roofs, Gothic spires. Damp-gray stone hidden by ivy but if you look closely you see how much of the ivy is dead, desiccated. Brittle and brown rattling in the wind.

Great aged oaks buttressed by stakes. Secured by wires. And a foot-high wrought-iron fence surrounding.

You see how the ruling class maintains its dominance by such buttressing, such security. Where otherwise, with others of us, a "natural" death is allowed.

"Alida! I think you have something to confess to."

Sternly Professor Schrader addresses me. The name "Alida" is an ax slash in her mouth and I am frozen with fear.

"What—what do you mean? Confess to—what?"

172

"I think you know, my dear. Perfectly well."

"Know—what?"

Professor Schrader is teasing, I think. Blocking my way with her obese figure as I prepare to run up the stairs. Breathing, panting in my face.

Close by, Candace Durstt looks on, quivering with intensity.

"Did you think that I would not *know?* That I have not ways of *knowing* your deviousness?"

"But—what have I done?"

My face throbs with heat. My voice shakes guiltily. Though I am not guilty of misbehaving yet I am suffused with guilt.

Professor Schrader's eyes are cunning behind the thick lenses of her glasses. Her elfin face is flushed with spite.

"You consort with unclean persons, Alida. You are risking the health of others with whom you live in intimate circumstances—namely, Candace and myself. In the rental contract you signed, you promised *cleanness.* You promised *community standards of decent behavior.* And so, I must ask you to leave the premises, 'Alida.' That is all."

"What do you mean—'leave the premises'? Why?"

"According to the rental contract you signed, your landlord is not required to explain grounds for eviction. This is a private residence, it is not the property of the University. *You* are to comply."

I am stammering now, trying to comprehend. *Cleanness*—have I not been *clean?* In what way have I been *unclean?*

Still, it is a sensation of guilt that sweeps through me. Though (I am sure) I have done nothing wrong.

Candace, who has been listening avidly, shrinks a little now, abashed. But she will not defend me against this terrible woman, I know.

"What I will do for you, 'AlidaLucash,' is this: I will not report you to the University housing office, which would disqualify you from living in other University-approved housing; and I will not report you to the Dean of the School of General Studies, which might result in your being suspended from the University for a semester. Untrustworthy and devious as you are, still I will not accelerate your self-destruction."

Professor Schrader presses a hand against her pendulous bosom, breathing audibly.

"But—please—tell me what have I done?"

"Enough! You know exactly what you have done. Like your friend before you—you have violated a trust."

Your friend before you. This can only mean *the drowned girl.*

It seems to me very cruel, yet in a way comprehensible, that the Professor should want to evict us both.

In a daze I climb to the second floor, and begin

to pack my things. It is devastating to me, to be turned out onto Humboldt Street in such a way. No warning!

Yet, it is not such a surprise, is it? With a part of my mind, I have been rehearsing this.

By nighttime I've found a room to rent at virtually the same rent as my room in Professor Schrader's house—in *The Magellan*. For it seems that Miri Krim's room has remained vacant since her departure.

To me, my life hasn't really started yet. One of my dreams is of a large baby with shut eyes like blind eyes and a recessed nose like the nose of a little pig and thin lips like a slit and (I think) this baby is meant to be me for it has not yet lived—it is waiting to live.

3.

Her room. Now, mine.

Sleep! Sleep, and be healed.

And take my hand for you are no longer alone.

In *The Magellan,* in room 2D, there is a single window overlooking Humboldt Street. Across the way is a brownstone building resembling *The Magellan*, with a water tank just visible on its roof.

I have not (yet) seen the water tank on the roof of *The Magellan* (though I have seen photographs of it online).

I am happy in my new room. I am not so lonely here, I think.

Here, there is a (small) (private) bathroom. An enormous improvement over the shared bathroom in the "family" house on Humboldt Street.

Still, I am careful about germs, bacteria. I am careful about the toilet seat. The sink, that is permanently stained; the shower stall, with the dripping showerhead.

Careful to examine the water, that comes out of the faucet as if reluctantly. Not gushing-hot but lukewarm, or cold.

How crowded it is, this Thursday evening at the University Medical Clinic!

Familiar faces! Frightened eyes.

Lying on my side. Shut eyes. Close hand into fist. Take a deep breath. Slow exhale.

Many questions have not been answered by investigating detectives. For instance, how did *the drowned girl* manage to gain access to the roof of *The Magellan* when the door to the stairs leading to the roof is always kept locked; and how did a girl weighing scarcely one hundred pounds manage to lift the heavy cover to the water tank, that required two men to lift it? How could she possibly have climbed inside the tank, and lowered the cover over herself? *Why would she have removed her clothes? And what has become of her clothes?*

The manager of *The Magellan* insisted that the door to the roof is always kept locked and that it was locked at the time of Miri Krim's disappearance. Custodial staff in the building were interviewed at length by detectives and not one of them was arrested.

"A key could be duplicated"—this is my suggestion.

One of the roof keys was stolen, and duplicated in a hardware store; the original was returned, and no one knew it had ever been taken. Armed with this key, the individual or individuals who abducted, raped and murdered Miri Krim could unlock the door to the stairs at any time, and bring their victim up to the roof to murder and dispose of her body.

Keys are duplicated all the time. Even those keys clearly marked *Do Not Duplicate.*

Some commandments are not enforced. Because unenforceable.

It was claimed, physical evidence had deteriorated in the water tank. Which was why (of course) the drowned girl had been brought to such a place by her abductor or abductors.

It was believed, in some quarters, that the

coroner botched the autopsy deliberately. For why otherwise was the rape kit "lost."

The coroner's finding is that the drowned girl died as a suicide or "accidentally" in the water tank—as if the victim had decided to go swimming one night in the tank with the heavy cover lowered over her, and was unable to get out again!

Removing all of her clothes. Making herself naked, exposed to jeering eyes.

And where are the clothes? Clothes removed from Miri Krim's body—where?

No one will ever be arrested, in the death of Miri Krim. Nothing will ever be resolved.

Something terrible will happen to us (again).

My math grade has risen: at mid-term, it is 46.

This is a considerable improvement over my dismal earlier grade. Almost miraculous.

Yet, it is a very low failing grade. It is far from the grade I require.

I have made an appointment to speak with the Professor.

I have rehearsed the words I will say to him— *I must earn an A in this course. If I do not maintain an A average, I will be dropped from the student loan program.*

I cannot afford even the interest on the loan(s).

I will not be allowed into the pre-med program which is my reason for coming to the University.

Please suggest ways I can raise my test scores,
Professor.
I am willing to work, work, work. I am willing to
do anything, I will be your slave.
(Just joking, Professor!)
Thank you, Professor!

Quickly, I ran through the underpass. Bodies lay
wrapped in rags festering like grave clothes.

You'd think—*Just bundles of old rags. Don't*
look.

But if you look, if you pause to see, to listen, to
smell—you realize that these are living beings,
human beings in layers of clothing, filthy
blankets. One bloated man rolled inside a garbage
bag. His head is shaved, his face is a cartoon
face with a dark O for a mouth. Smelling of stale
sweat and much worse.

Heyyyy missy!

I did not hear. Heart beating too loud in my ears.

—*need help standing. Get to my feet. Thank*
you, dear! Please.

At the steps poised to run up into the daylight
where I can breathe. And the words come to me,
it is Miri Krim who whispers in my ear *Even as*
you have done unto the least of these, you have
done unto me.

And so, I returned to help the bloated man,
wrapped in a garbage bag, and reeking of his
body, to his (swollen, unsteady) feet.

I did not make an appointment to see the math Professor.

I did make an appointment with the University Medical Clinic Blood Unit.

It is Thursday evening. Something seems to be wrong.

The procedure has been altered. At first, I am instructed by an attendant to lie down, on my side, as in the past; but no attendant comes to take my blood. At least five minutes pass, very uncomfortably.

Then, I am being asked to sit up. The fluorescent lighting is unpleasantly bright.

A medical worker, an Asian woman, has appeared. She smiles at me hesitantly. Her eyes are wary, cautious. Her smile is a cautious smile that scarcely distends her mouth.

Choosing her words with care as with a tweezers she might pick broken glass out of an open, festering wound.

"I'm afraid—Miss Lucash—'Alida'—your blood work has come back positive for—"

It is not possible: HIV.

Or—is the woman's mouth shaping another word: hepatitis?

A roaring in my ears. The shuddering of water, dark rippling water, in the tank.

I am not hearing this. (Am I?) Sitting on the edge of the examination table I stare at the doctor with a hopeful smile.

• • •

Positive is not what you want to hear, in the matter of infectious diseases.

Negative is what you want to hear, in the matter of infectious diseases.

Questions are put to me regarding *sexual contacts, needle sharing.*

White-coated medical workers do not seem to believe me when I insist that I had had no *sexual contacts.* Still less, that I have not *shared needles* with *fellow addicts.*

By this time I am feeling very weak. It does seem clear, something is wrong with my blood—anemia?

How close, *anemia* and *amnesia.*

Which is cause, which is effect, is not known.

The examination room, which is not a large room, is crowded with white-coated persons by this time. Dr. Liu (for that is her name) is a presiding resident, the others are (younger) interns or medical students.

Though I answer the questions put to me by these individuals truthfully not one of my words, not a single syllable, sounds authentic or sincere. The more agitated I become, the more likely that I am lying; or, as Dr. Liu suggests—"Confabulating."

I am regarded with pity, sympathy, dismay, disapproval. My voice is hoarse with the desperation of a guilty person who has been found out, exposed in ignominy like a rat in a cage, a rat injected with disease, blinking foolishly at its tormentors.

I tell them I would like to come back another day, and take the blood test again. I have not been feeling well lately, and have not been sleeping well. I've been evicted from my rooming house and forced to move to an apartment building that, just the previous year, had been shut down by the Hudson County Board of Health.

I have not slept well in weeks. I have had very little appetite.

I have shared a bathroom with unclean persons. I have eaten and drunk food that has been— possibly—tainted; I have not been able to escape drinking water that might be *impure*.

All this may have affected my blood work. Isn't this possible?

Dr. Liu stares at me as if uncertain how to reply. "Oh—yes. It is possible."

From the custodian's closet-sized room in the basement of *The Magellan* I have taken the (crucial) key to the roof.

At the hardware store on Pitcairn and Mercer, I have had the key duplicated.

(Does it matter to the bored clerk that it is stamped on the key *Do Not Duplicate?*—it does not.)

At a time when no one will observe me, when the custodian is emptying trash barrels into the Dumpster in the alley, I will return the original key to the drawer in his custodian's closet-sized room.

In silence Professor Gee hands the seventeen-page paper to me. As I fumble to take it from him I see, to my shock, that there is a grade of A on the cover page in bright red ink.

Except, when I look more closely, the grade is not A but A? Seeing that I am unable to speak Professor Gee says with a cold smile, "Very good work, Miss Lucash! In fact, it is quite unlike any term paper on the subject of 'memory' which I have ever received from an undergraduate at this University. That's to say—in twenty-two years."

My hands are shaking with excitement, yet dread. I have broken out into a cold, sickish sweat. A part of me wants to smile happily, to think—*But this is what I deserve, at last! I have worked so hard.*

Yet, there is no mistaking the ? affixed to the grade. There is no mistaking the chill that exudes from Professor Gee—(who is quite the witty lecturer in front of an audience)— and the reason that he has summoned me to his office in one of the Gothic towers of the University's Psychology Department.

"You see, it is an A paper—uncontestably. And

yet, I am obliged to question: is this A paper the work of 'AlidaLucash'? Entirely—*hers?*"

In the Professor's face an expression of muted disdain, contempt—*Of course, I expect nothing more of you than this. You and your kind disgust me.*

I tell the Professor yes, yes I wrote the paper myself.

"Speak up, Miss Lucash. What did you say?"

"I—I wrote the p-paper myself. . . ."

In my mouth, which has gone suddenly dry, these words are obviously fraudulent. It is no wonder that Professor Gee stares at me with something like hatred.

Yet, when Professor Gee speaks he is polite, even thoughtful. There is even something playful in his tone.

"I would like to see your notes for this ambitious paper, Miss Lucash. And if you have early drafts of the paper, I would like to see them as well."

I am feeling very strange. In the hard-backed chair facing the Professor across his desk, making every effort not to be upset, or hurt, that the Professor has accused me of—cheating? theft? plagiarism?

In a weak voice I say: "Yes."

But my notes are lost, I think. Early drafts of my term paper have disappeared into my (defective) laptop. I am not sure if I saved them correctly after completing and printing out the paper, with numerous missteps, on a (defective) printer.

"Or, you can summarize your paper for me now. Present it, as a little lecture. I am particularly impressed with your footnotes, Miss Lucash. Daring of you to quote sources at odds with 'Herman Gee.' "

I have become flushed and confused. That footnote, near the end of the paper, was one that I'd taken out, and restored; taken out again, and restored; for after thinking it over I'd concluded that Herman Gee would find such evidence contradicting his own work on memory (as he has presented it this semester in his lectures) stimulating and interesting, and not a "threat" to his professional reputation—though perhaps, seeing the set of the man's jaw, I had been naïve about this.

Hesitantly, in my hopeful voice, I begin to summarize the paper. As Professor Gee stares at me I become hopelessly confused. (Am I allowed to glance at it? I wonder. It would be helpful to read certain of the more difficult passages aloud in order to explicate them.) Mercifully, after less than sixty seconds Professor Gee interrupts me.

"Very well. Thank you, Miss Lucash. I see you have successfully memorized certain of the passages."

I am not sure what to do. What is expected of me.

Confess! You are dishonest.

You are unworthy of the University, you do not belong here.

It is not true that I have plagiarized the paper —"A Biological Theory of Memory." Much research has gone into the preparation of the paper. One hundred hours at the least, in the University library.

Yet, a terrible sick guilt suffuses me. I am feeling very tired. I am laughing nervously, which seems to startle and annoy the Professor.

"Well. Enough. Let me reiterate—I am requesting that you print out your notes and early drafts, and bring them to me, here in this office, by tomorrow noon. Failure to comply will mean failure in the course and the likelihood of your being summoned before the University disciplinary committee."

I will not be able to comply. There is no way for me to comply. My heart feels like a sponge that has been squeezed, a filthy kitchen sponge.

Yet, cravenly I nod at the Professor—"Yes, Professor Gee. I will try."

She slips the key into my fingers. Between my fingers, gripped tight.

With this key, I unlock the door at the end of the third-floor corridor of The Magellan, *that leads to the roof.*

On the stairs, she precedes me. A shadow, quicksilver!

Come with me! Hurry—*she is murmuring.*

It is surprising to me: stepping out onto the roof, so close to the (nighttime, overcast) sky. A gust of wind bringing tears to my eyes.

On the roof, I approach the water tank gigantic as a mountain.

Surprising too, how familiar the rooftop is. The water tank, and the metal ladder rising against the side of the water tank.

Though the smell here of creosote and fresh, harsh air is not familiar. Closeness of the sky layered with clouds like putty spread by a trowel but glowering with phosphorescence.

In the distance, on the farther side of the New York Central train tracks, the long hill to the University, that is not visible by night except as a string of street lights; and at the top of the hill the bell tower like a blank staring mad eye.

Climb the ladder! Hurry—*she is murmuring.*

A sudden unexpected strength flows into my arms and legs as I grip the ladder and climb. For a moment I feel dizzy—but only for a moment. Clearly I am not enfeebled—my blood is not "infected."

At the top of the ladder, using every ounce of strength in my upper arms and shoulders, I hope to be capable of lifting the heavy cover—if but for a few desperate seconds.

My heart is full to bursting. Suffused with happiness in this strange place.

A touch on my shoulder, and I turn—but there is no one. (The wind?)

For a moment there is the danger that I might let go of the ladder—a wave of vertigo returns, weakening my knees.

In the distance, the luminous bell tower.

Is there a bell tolling? What is the hour? Straining my eyes, I can't see the clock face—I can't hear the tolling.

Ten o'clock? Eleven? Midnight?

There is the danger that I will not be strong enough to lift the cover after all—for there is no one to help me.

A danger that I might let go of the ladder, and fall to the roof fifteen feet below, and not be found until morning, or later, when my feeble cries are heard by a stranger passing on Humboldt Street.

I have decided to leave the University. I will move out of *The Magellan* without giving notice.

My rental deposit will not be returned to me. But this is a small price to pay for my life.

The beautiful old University, I will remember. The long hill to the Hall of Languages, the bell tower at the top of the hill, the tolling of (invisible) bells.

THE SITUATIONS
1. Kittens

Daddy was driving us home. Three of us in the back seat and Lula who was his favorite in the passenger's seat.

Lula cried Oh Daddy!—look.

At the side of the road, in broken grasses, was something small and furry-white, that appeared to be alive.

Oh Daddy *please*.

Daddy laughed. Daddy braked the car to a stop. Lula jumped out of the car. We ran back with her, to discover in the broken grasses three small kittens—white, with black and russet markings.

We picked up the kittens! They were so tiny, fitting in the palms of our hands, weighing only a few ounces! Each was mewing, its eyes scarcely open. Oh, oh!—we'd never seen anything so wonderful in our lives! We ran back to the car where Daddy was waiting, to beg Daddy to take them home with us.

At first Daddy said no. Daddy said the kittens would make messes in the car.

Lula said Oh Daddy *please*. We all promised to clean up any messes the kittens made.

So Daddy gave in. Daddy loved Lula best,

but we were happy to be Daddy's children, too.

In the back seat we had two of the little kittens. In the front, Lula was holding the whitest kitten.

We were so excited! So happy with the kittens! Lula said she would call the whitest kitten Snowflake, and we said we would call our little kittens Pumpkin and Cinder because Pumpkin had orange splotches in his white fur, and Cinder had black splotches in his white fur.

For some minutes Daddy drove in silence. We did all the chattering! You could hear tiny mews, if you listened hard.

Then, Daddy said, Do I smell a mess?

We cried No, no!

I think I smell a mess.

No Daddy!

Three messes. I smell them.

No Daddy!

(And this was so: none of the kittens had made messes.)

But Daddy braked the car to a stop. At the bridge over the river where there is a steep ramp, outside our town and about two miles from our house, Daddy parked the car and said to Lula, Give me Snowflake, and Daddy squinted at us in the rearview mirror and said, Give me Pumpkin, and give me Cinder.

We began to cry. Lula cried loudest. But Daddy grabbed the little kitten from her, and reached into the back seat red-faced and frowning to grab Pumpkin and Cinder from us. We were not strong enough and we were not brave enough to keep Daddy from taking the kittens from us, in Daddy's big hand. The kittens were mewing loudly by this time and quivering in terror.

Daddy left the car and with big Daddy-strides climbed the ramp to the bridge and threw the kittens over the railing. Three tiny things rising at first against the misty sky, then quickly falling, and gone.

When Daddy returned to the car Lula cried, Daddy *why*?

Daddy said, Because I am Daddy, who decides how things end.

2. Feral Kiss

In secret, by foot, he traveled to the Mainland. He lived on an island of approximately eight square miles, boot-shaped like Italy. Between the Island and the Mainland was a two-mile floating bridge. His parents had forbidden him to journey to the Mainland; the Mainland was the "easy, slack life"; the Island was the life of discipline, severity, God's will. His parents had broken off ties with their relatives who lived on the Mainland, who in turn pitied the Islanders as uneducated, superstitious, and impoverished.

On the Island there were colonies of feral cats, much inbred, ferocious if cornered or trapped, but surpassingly beautiful—one of the colonies was comprised predominantly of flamey-orange tiger cats with six toes, another was predominantly midnight-black cats with tawny eyes, another was predominantly white, long-haired cats with glaring green eyes, and another, the largest colony, predominantly tortoiseshell cats with intricate stone-colored, silver, and black markings, and golden eyes, seemed to thrive in a rough, rock-strewn area near the floating bridge. It was generally forbidden for Island children to approach the feral cats, or to feed them; it was dangerous for anyone to approach the cats in the hope of petting them, still less capturing one of them and bringing it home; even small kittens were known to scratch and bite furiously. Yet, on his way to the Mainland, as he approached the floating bridge, he couldn't resist tossing bits of food to the tortoiseshell cats who regarded him from a little distance with flat, hostile eyes—Kitty? *Kitty?* Such beautiful creatures! One day brashly he managed to seize hold of a young tortoiseshell cat scarcely more than a kitten, very thin, with prominent ribs and high, alert ears, and for a moment he held its quivering life in his fingers like his own heart seized out of his chest— then the cat squirmed frantically, hissed, scratched and sank its small sharp teeth into the flesh at the base of his thumb, he released it with a little cry *Damn!* and wiped the blood on his pant leg, and continued on his journey across the floating bridge.

On the Mainland, he saw her: a girl he imagined to be his own age, or a little younger, walking with other children. The coastal wind was shrouded with mist, damply cold, relentless. Droplets of moisture had formed on his eyelashes like tears. Her long hair whipped in the wind. Her perfect face was turned from him in shyness, or in coyness. He'd grown daring, brash; his experience with the tortoiseshell cat hadn't discouraged but seemed to have encouraged him. He was a boy pretending to be a man here on the Mainland, where he felt to himself older, more confident. And here, no one knew his name, or the name of his family. He walked with the girl, drawing her away from the other children. He asked to know her name—*Mariana*. He held her small hand, that resisted his initially, as he clutched at it. He kissed her on the lips, lightly yet with much excitement. When she didn't draw away he kissed her again, with more force. She turned aside as if to run from him. But he clutched her hand, and her arm; he gripped her tight, and kissed her so hard, he felt the imprint of her teeth against his. It seemed that she was kissing him in return, though less forcefully. She pulled away. She snatched his hand and, laughing, bit him on the inside of the thumb, the soft flesh at the base of the thumb.

In astonishment he stared at the quick-flowing blood. The wound was so small and yet—so much blood! His pant legs were stained. His boots were splattered. He retreated, and the girl ran to catch up with the other children—all of them running together, he saw now, along the wide, rough beach littered with storm debris, their laughter high-pitched and taunting and not one of them glanced back.

Gripped suddenly by a fear that the bridge had floated away, he returned to the floating bridge. But there it remained, buffeted by coastal winds, and looking smaller, and more weathered. It was late autumn. He could not recall the season in which he'd started out—had it been summer? Spring? The sea lifted in angry churning waves. The Island was near-invisible behind a shroud of mist. In the waves, he saw the faces of his older, Island kin. Gray-bearded men, frowning women. He was breathless returning to the Island across the rocking, floating bridge. At shore he paid no heed to the colony of tortoiseshell cats that seemed to be awaiting him with small taunting mews and sly cat faces, amid the rocks. The wound at the base of his thumb hurt; he was ashamed of his injury, the perceptible marks of small sharp teeth in his flesh. Within a few days the wound became livid, and with a fishing knife cauterized in flame he reopened the wound, to let the blood flow hotly again. He wrapped the base of his thumb in a bandage. He explained that he'd injured himself carelessly on a rusted nail or hook. He returned to his life that soon swept over him like waves rising onto the beach, streaming through the rocks. There would be a day when he removed the bandage, and saw the tiny serrated scar in the flesh, all but healed. In secret, he would kiss the scar in a swoon of emotion but in time, he would cease to remember why.

3. Hope

Daddy was driving us home. Just two of us in the back seat and Esther who was Daddy's favorite, in the passenger's seat.

Esther cried Oh Daddy!—look out!

A dark-furry creature was crossing the road in front of Daddy's car, legs moving rapidly. It might have been a large cat, or a young fox. Daddy did not slacken his speed for an instant— he did not turn the wheel or brake the car to avoid hitting the creature but he did not appear to press down on the gas pedal to strike it deliberately.

The right front wheel struck it with a small thud.

There was a sharp little cry, then silence.

Oh Daddy *please. Please stop.*

Esther's voice was thin and plaintive and though it was a begging sort of voice, it was a voice without hope.

Daddy laughed. Daddy did not brake the car to a stop.

In the back we knelt on the seat to peer out the rear window—seeing, in the broken grasses at the side of the road, the furry creature writhing in agony.

Daddy—stop! Daddy please stop, the animal is *hurt*.

But our voices were thin and plaintive and without hope and Daddy paid little heed to us but continued driving and humming to himself and in the front seat Esther was crying in her soft helpless way and in the back seat we were very quiet.

One of us whispered to the other *That was a kitty!*

The other whispered *That was a fox!*

At the bridge over the river where there's a steep ramp Daddy braked the car to a stop. Daddy was frowning and irritable, and Daddy said to Esther, Get out of the car. And Daddy turned grunting to us in the back seat and Daddy's eyes were glaring-angry as he told us to get out of the car.

We were very frightened. Yet, there was no place to hide in the back of Daddy's car.

Outside, Esther was shivering. A chill wind blew from the mist-shrouded river. We huddled with Esther as Daddy approached.

In Daddy's face there was regret, and remorse.

But it was remorse for something that had not yet happened, and could not be avoided. Calmly Daddy struck Esther a blow to the back with his fist, that knocked her down like a shot, so breathless she couldn't scream or cry at first but lay on the ground quivering. We wanted to run away but dared not for Daddy's long legs would catch up with us, we knew.

Daddy struck us, one and then the other. One on the back, as Esther had been struck, and the other a glancing careless blow on the side of the head as if in this case (my case) the child was so hopeless, he was beyond disciplining. *Oh oh oh!*—we had learned to stifle our cries.

In long Daddy-strides Daddy returned to the car to smoke a cigarette. This had happened before but not quite in this way and so when a thing happens in a way resembling a prior way it is more upsetting than if it had not happened before, ever in any way. On the lumpy ground in broken and desiccated grasses we lay sobbing, trying to catch our breaths. Esther who was the oldest recovered first, crawled to Kevin and me and helped us sit up, and stand on our shaky stick legs. We were dazed with pain and also with the sick sensation that comes to you when you have not expected something to happen as it did but, as it begins to happen, you remember that you have in fact experienced it before, and this fact determines, in the way of a sequence of bolts locking a sequence of doors, the certitude that it will recur.

In the car Daddy sat smoking. The driver's door was open partway but still the car was filling with bluish smoke like mist.

Between Esther and Daddy there was a situation unique to Esther and Daddy, as it had once been unique to Lula and Daddy: if Esther had disappointed Daddy, and had been punished for disappointing Daddy, Esther was allowed, perhaps even expected, to refer to this punishment provided Esther did not challenge Daddy, or disappoint Daddy further. A clear, simple question posted by Esther to Daddy often seemed, to our surprise, to be welcomed.

Esther said, a catch in her throat, Oh Daddy *why*?

Daddy said, Because I am Daddy, whose children must never give up hope.

GREAT BLUE HERON

That cry! Hoarse, not-human, fading almost at once. But in an instant she has been wakened.

The cry came from the lake, she supposes. Owls. Waterfowl on the lake—loons, geese, mallards. Through the night in her uneasy sleep she hears their beautiful forlorn cries, that are usually muted like human voices heard at a distance. Sometimes there is an agitation on the water, what sounds like a frantic flapping of wings—she listens acutely hoping not to hear cries of distress.

Too early for her to wake. Too early to be *conscious*.

She has been exhausted lately, sleep is precious to her.

Her nightgown is unpleasantly damp from perspiration. The bedclothes are damp. She is breathing quickly, thinly. The cry from the lake has unnerved her—it did not sound human yet it is familiar to her.

She whispers her husband's name. She doesn't want to wake him but she is feeling anxious, lonely.

The bed is larger than she recalls. Almost, she isn't sure if her husband is there, at the farther (left) edge of the bed.

But he is there, seemingly asleep. His broad naked back to her.

Gently she eases against him, craving the touch of another. The protective arms of another.

Her husband appears to be sleeping undisturbed. Whatever the cry from the lake, he has not been wakened.

He has thrown off most of the covers, his shoulders and upper back are cool to the touch. Without opening his eyes he turns sleepily to her, to close his arms around her.

Strong and protective the husband's arms. And his deep slow breathing a kind of protection as well. She lays her head beside his, on a corner of his pillow. In his sleep the husband does strange, sculptural things with pillows: bends them in two, sets them beneath his head vertically, merges two pillows into one, lies at an uncomfortable angle with his head crooked. Yet he sleeps soundly, the nocturnal birds rarely wake him.

Husband and wife are very comfortable together. Without needing to speak they communicate perfectly in their bed in the dark. The wife will claim that she is a light sleeper yet often she falls asleep close to the husband in this way, sharing just the edge of his pillow.

It is the purest sleep, sharing the edge of the husband's pillow.

Close about the roof of the house are smaller birds. Cardinals are the first to wake at dawn.

Their familiar, sweet calls are tentative, like questions. They are asking *What is this? Where are we? What will be expected of us?* It must be terrifying to be a bird, she thinks. You must forage for food every minute, you must never rest or your small heart will cease beating.

You must fly, you must exert your wings. Frail bones, that can be snapped so easily. Yet these bones are strong enough to lift you into the air and to buoy you aloft through your life.

These are the birds of day—birds whose songs are familiar to the ear. On the lake and in the marshy land bordering the lake are larger birds, mysterious birds, that cry, call, hoot, moan, shriek, murmur, and make quavering noises, harsh manic laughter through the night.

The screech owl, a singular shuddering cry.

The great blue heron, a hoarse croak of a cry.

Take my hand. And take care.

Hand in hand they are walking along the edge of the lake. The earth underfoot is soft, spongy. It is a chill May morning. Color is bleached from the earth as from the sky. Tall grasses at the water's shore appear to be broken, trampled. There is a smell of wet rotted leaves. Though the season is spring it is a twilit time and all that she sees appears to be neither wholly alive nor wholly dead.

She is gripping her husband's hand just slightly tighter than usual. Perhaps the husband is limping—just slightly. It is natural for the wife to weave her fingers through the husband's fingers. He is the stronger of the two, she defers to him even in the matter of walking together. Soon after they'd met they began holding hands in this way and that was many years ago but in this twilight hour at the lake the wife is unable to calculate how long. A strange silence has come upon her like a veil tied tight against her mouth.

Come here! Look.

Carefully the husband leads the wife. Nearly hidden among tall grasses and cattails at the shore is what appears to be a little colony of nesting ducks—mallards.

These are the most common local ducks. The wife recognizes the sleek dark-green head of the male, the plain brown feathers of the female.

A light rain is falling, causing the surface of the lake to shiver like the skin of a living creature. The sun doesn't seem to be rising in the east so much as materializing behind banks of cloud—pale, without color, sheer light.

She is gripping her husband's hand. She thinks —*We have never been so happy.*

Has he brought her here, to tell her this? *Why* has he brought her here?

The lake at this hour appears different than it appears by day. It seems larger, lacking boundaries. Columns of mist rise, like exhaled breaths. By day you can see individual trees but in this dusk all is shadow like a smear of thick paint. And the surface of the lake reflecting only a dull metallic sheen.

A sun so hazy-pale, it might be the moon. (*Is that the moon?*) Obscured by clouds that appear to be unmoving, fixed in place.

There is something melancholy, the wife thinks, in such beauty. For the lake is beautiful, even drained of color. It is one of the beautiful places of her life, it has become precious to her. Though it is not a large lake in the mountains, only a semi-rural, semi-suburban lake of less than two miles in circumference, at its deepest no more than fifteen feet and much of the water near shore shallow, clotted with cattails.

It is difficult to walk along the lake, there is no single trail amid dense underbrush. Especially dense are stretches of *Rosa acicularis*, thorny wild rose that catch in clothing and raise bleeding scratches on unprotected skin.

Hand in hand walking along the shore. They have come to the end of their property and are making their way along a faint trail in the marsh. The wife is shivering, her feet are getting wet, she would like to turn back but the husband presses forward, he has something to show her. Through their long marriage it is the husband who has had much to show the wife.

Above the lake are flashes of lightning, sound-less.

On the steel-colored lake are shadow figures: a flotilla of Canada geese. The husband and wife stand very still observing the large handsome gray-feathered geese as they float on the surface of the water, heads tucked beneath their wings like illustrations in a children's storybook.

All is serene, near-motionless as in a dream.

Then, seemingly out of nowhere, about twenty feet away, there appears a curious long-legged creature making its way along the shore, in the direction of the mallard nests.

The wife stares, appalled. It is a great blue heron, a predator bird, very thin, with a long snaky neck and scaly legs, a long sharp beak. Eerie and unsettling that the thing, the creature, makes no attempt to use its wings to fly but simply walks awkwardly, yet rapidly, like a human being in some way handicapped or disfigured.

Before any of the mallards sight the predator it attacks the nearest nest. Its beak stabs pitilessly, with robotic precision. There is a violent struggle, there are shrieks, a frenzied flapping of mallard wings as the heron stabs at the nest, piercing eggs with its bill; within seconds it has gobbled down mallard eggs, brazen and indifferent to the smaller waterfowl hissing and flapping their wings in protest.

At another nest the heron discovers tiny unfledged ducklings. The affrighted mallard parents are unable to interfere as the tall snaky-necked bird lifts ducklings one by one in its bill, swiftly, and swallows them whole.

By now all the mallards are protesting, shrieking. There must be two dozen mallards aroused to alarm. Some are on land, at the shore; others are flailing about in the water. Their cries are *cwak-cwak-cwak*, emitted in fury and despair. But the cries come too late. The alarm is ineffectual. The great blue heron remains unmoved, indifferent. Within a minute it has eaten its fill and now lifts its wide gray-feathered wings, extends its leathery-looking neck, and flies away across the lake with a horrible sort of composure.

Only now does the predator emit a cry—harsh, hoarse, croaking—triumphant-sounding, grating to the ear.

Oh God!—she is waking now.

Now, her eyes are open, stark and blind. So surprised, she can't see at first.

For long minutes unable to move as her heart pounds. Stunned as if her body, in the region of her heart, has been pierced by the predator bird's long sharp beak.

She wills herself to wake fully. It is a conscious, moral decision, she thinks—to *wake fully.*

Throws aside the bedclothes that are stifling to her, removes her nightgown, damp with sweat, and tosses it onto the floor like a disgraced thing.

The bed beside her is empty. Of course, the bed is empty.

It is three weeks and two days since her husband's death.

He has left. He has gone. He will not be returning.
These words she tells herself a dozen times a day. These words that are the flattest recitation of horror yet somehow cannot be wholly comprehended. Thus, she must repeat.
He has left. He has gone. He will not be returning.

A jangling at the front door. There is no keeping the intruder out.

Not a predator bird but a scavenger bird. Hunched shoulders like deformed wings, rapacious bright eyes that move over the widow like hunger.

"You will want to sell this property. Of course."
No. I do not want to sell this property.
Gravely the brother-in-law speaks. Though she has told the brother-in-law that it is too soon after the husband's death to think of such matters.

". . . always said, the property is really too much for just two people. And now . . ."

He'd stood on the front stoop ringing the bell. Calling *Claudia! Clau-dia! It's me.*

And who, she wonders, is *me?*

What has she to do with this *me?*

She could not keep the brother-in-law out of the house. She could not run away to hide upstairs for he would have called 911 to report a desperate woman in (possible) danger of harming herself or worse yet he'd have broken into the house to find her, in triumph.

Saying then—*Poor Claudia! I may have saved her life.*

It is all beyond her control. What people say about her now that her husband has died.

It is astonishing: the (uninvited, unwanted) brother-in-law is sitting in the living room of this house in which he has not (ever) been a guest without the presence of his brother.

The first time (ever) that the brother-in-law has been alone with his brother's wife who has long been wary of him— his glistening eyes, too-genial smile.

The brother-in-law has even helped himself to a drink—amber-colored whiskey splashed into a glass, from a bottle kept in a cabinet with a very few other, select bottles of liquor. The brother-in-law has asked if the widow will join him in a drink and the widow has declined with a nervous smile. How strange, to be asked to join an unwanted intruder in a drink, and to murmur *No thank you* in your own house.

A numbed sense of horror is rising in the widow, of all that she has relinquished and lost.

In his earnest salesman's voice the brother-in-law is speaking of planning for the future, the widow's future. She is the executrix of the husband's estate which involves a good deal of responsibility, and "expertise"—which the widow does not have, understandably.

"I can help you, Claudia. Of course . . ."

How strange, her name on this man's lips— *Claudia.* Worse, he sometimes calls her *Claudie.* As if there were a special intimacy between them.

The brother-in-law speaks of "finances"— "taxes"—"lakeside property"—as if he is being forced to utter painful truths. As if this visit is not his choice (not at all!) but his responsibility as the (younger) brother of the deceased husband, the (concerned, caring) brother-in-law of the widow.

Politely, stiffly the widow is listening.

In truth, the widow is not listening.

Only dimly does the widow hear the brother-in-law speak for there is a roaring in her ears as of a distant waterfall. Only vaguely is she aware of the mouth moving. A kind of hinge to the mouth, like that of a scavenger bird.

Why is he here? Why is he here *with her?* This person in all of the world whom she has never trusted. This person who she believes borrowed money from her husband with the tacit understanding on both sides that the money would (probably) not be returned.

The brother-in-law who has expressed an awkward, unwished-for interest in her as if there were a kind of complicity between them. *You know—that I know—you will never tell Jim.*

Jim! But the husband was called *James.*

Except at times by the younger brother. With a smirking smile—*Jim.* Worse yet, *Jimmy.*

But this is so: she'd never told her husband how his younger brother has had a habit of standing uncomfortably close to her, looming his bulky body over her; he leans his face into hers, hugging her too tightly in greeting or in farewell, so that she is made to feel the unpleasant solidity and heat of his (male) body. How he addresses her in an undertone with a suggestive smile—*H'lo Claudie. Been missing you.*

Often, at family gatherings, the brother-in-law's breath smells of whiskey. Warm, gaseous. And his heavy hand falling on her arm as if accidentally.

She has never told her husband. She would have been embarrassed and ashamed to tell her husband. Rather she would keep a disagreeable secret to herself than share it and disturb others.

Her love for her husband had been a protective love, which she did not want to jeopardize. She did not want to be the bearer of upsetting news to her kindly, sweet-natured and trusting husband and had kept many things from him in the long years of their marriage.

She would keep from him now, if she could, the rawness of her grief. She would not want the (deceased) husband to know how she misses him.

She would not want the (deceased) husband to know how she distrusts, dislikes, fears his brother.

In any case (she has told herself) nothing is likely to happen between her and the brother-in-law because she would not allow it to happen.

"You're looking very pale, Claudia. We all hope you're getting enough sleep."

At this she smiles ironically. *Enough sleep!* There could be only *enough sleep* if she shut her eyes forever.

"Sure I can't fix you a drink? I think I'll have another—just a little. . . ."

The brother-in-law is in his mid-fifties, several years younger than the (deceased) husband and of the widow's approximate age. He has made a show of being a devoted family man but his life has been carefully arranged so that he spends as little time with his family as possible. Solid-bodied, big-armed, despite his slightly hunched shoulders he has a ruddy golfer's face and the manner of one eager to *take charge* with his very hands if necessary.

The widow can see the hands *getting a grip*—on her.

As if she were a golf club. An instrument to be deftly deployed by one who will *take charge*.

"The real estate market isn't great at the present time—I acknowledge that. Mortgage rates are high. But with careful marketing, and sound investments after the sale of the property . . ."

The brother-in-law's eyes are damp, inquisitive. Moving over the widow's body like swarming ants as he pours himself another drink, and drinks.

". . . of course, it has been a terrible shock. You have had a *trauma*. Which is why . . ."

The brother-in-law is confident that he will win over the widow. Her silence is a goad to his ingenuity. Her politeness, her courtesy, her habit of deference are a goad to his loquacity. It isn't clear to him—it isn't clear that it much matters—whether the widow is near-catatonic with grief or is simply stiff-backed with female stubbornness in opposition to him precisely because he has the very best advice to give to her.

That is how women are—perverse!

In his professional life the brother-in-law has been an investment banker. He is not an investment banker now—(the widow isn't sure if he "has his own business" or is "between jobs")—}but he retains the skills, the information, the experience of investment banking or at least the insider vocabulary, and he is after all the widow's brother-in-law, to whom the widow might naturally turn in this time of distress.

(Indeed the widow has been behaving strangely since the husband's death: keeping to herself, avoiding even her family, her closest relatives and friends. Avoiding *him*.)

"You know, Jim would want you to confide in me. He'd want you to bring me any questions you have about the estate, finances, death taxes, IRS taxes, putting the house on the market. . . ."

But I do not want to put the house on the market.

He will be happy to take on the responsibility of acting as the executor of her husband's estate, the brother-in-law says. If she wishes. Naming him executor in her place would require just a consultation with her lawyer. Such an arrangement is "very commonly done"—"a very good idea"—when a widow is inexperienced in "money matters" and has had a bad shock.

"Shall we make a date? An appointment? I can call your lawyer, we can set up a meeting early next week. . . ."

The widow scarcely seems to hear. It is true that she is very pale, waxy-pale, her skin exudes a kind of luminescence that makes her appear younger than her age, as her loose, somewhat disheveled hair, streaked with gray, silver, white hairs and falling to her shoulders, gives her a look some-where between despair and wild elation.

"I said, I'll call your lawyer and set up a meeting for us. . . ."

The widow is staring out a window, at the rear of the house; a short distance away, down a slight incline, the wind-rippled lake reflects the light of late afternoon.

"Claudia? Are you all right? You've been listening, I hope. . . ."

The brother-in-law's voice is edged with annoyance. The brother-in-law is not a man to be slighted. He is wearing an open-necked shirt of some fine, expensive material—Egyptian cotton perhaps. The shirt is a pale lavender as his cord trousers are a dark lavender. His shoes are canvas deck shoes. He makes it a point to be well dressed though his clothes are usually tight and he looks crammed inside them, like an ill-shaped sausage.

The widow recalls how, only a few days before her husband was stricken and hospitalized, the brother-in-law, at a family gathering, had approached her when she was alone and stood uncomfortably close to her, as if daring her to acknowledge his sexual interest and push past him.

Been missin you, Claudie. You're looking terrific.

Always, insultingly, the brother-in-law has felt obliged to comment on his brother's wife's appearance. As if there were some competition between the brothers' wives, of which the wives themselves were not aware.

Since the brother-in-law has gained access to the house, and has been sitting in the living room, repeating his rehearsed words to the widow, the widow has been observing the movement of waterfowl on the lake—ducks, geese. Predators have not gobbled down all of this season's ducklings and goslings. There are even several cygnets, for there is a pair of resident swans on the lake. Dazzling-white swans of surpassing beauty and calm.

When she is feeling very sad, very lonely and distraught, the widow escapes the house in which the telephone is likely to ring, and walks along the lake shore counting ducklings, goslings. Cygnets.

She has sometimes seen the great blue heron, a solitary hunter. By day, the heron does not seem quite so terrifying as it has seemed by night.

"Oh, there!"—the widow speaks excitedly seeing a large rail-thin bird lift its wings suddenly and rise into the air, with initial awkwardness, alone over the lake.

"What are you looking at, Claudia? What's out there that is so damned interesting?"—the brother-in-law turns to look over his shoulder, his chin creasing fatly.

The great blue heron is a prehistoric creature, of a strange and unsettling beauty. The widow stares entranced as slowly and with dignity the heron flies out of sight. But the brother-in-law doesn't seem to have seen.

"Well, that's quite a view. You're lucky, to have such a lakefront property. Jim had the right idea, this property is quite an investment. . . ."

The widow objects, more sharply than she'd intended: "James didn't think of it as an 'investment.' It was—it is—our home."

"Well, sure! I didn't mean . . ."

"We chose the house together. James and me. I think you know that. It wasn't the decision of just one of us."

"Right! No need to get upset, Claudia."

"I think—I think now that you should leave. I have many things to do. . . ."

It is maddening, the widow hears her apologetic voice. Though trembling with dislike of the intruder she feels she must speak to him in a tone of apology.

The brother-in-law smiles, half-jeering. " 'Many things to do'! Exactly, Claudia. Things you should certainly be doing, that I could help you with."

"No. I don't think so. . . ."

"What d'you mean, 'I don't think so.' Jim would be concerned about you, Claudia."

The widow is stung by the casual way in which the brother-in-law has been uttering her husband's name as if it were an ordinary name to be batted about as in a Ping-Pong game.

"No. I said—*no*."

The brother-in-law blinks at her, and raises his eyebrows, in a pretense of mild surprise. She is in danger of speaking shrilly. She is in danger of betraying emotion. She knows how closely the brother-in-law is observing her, how he will report to others. *Claudia is looking awful. Obviously she hasn't been sleeping. Hope she isn't drinking— secretly. Can't imagine what Jim was thinking of, naming that poor woman executrix of his estate!*

The visit is over. But the brother-in-law is slow to leave.

He has set down his whiskey glass, which he seems to have drained. His face is flushed and ruddy, the little ant-eyes gleam with a malicious sort of satisfaction, yet aggression. For the brother-in-law is one to want more, more.

On their way to the door the brother-in-law continues to speak. The widow is aware of his hands gesturing—always, the man's gestures are florid, exaggerated. He is a TV sort of person— he could be a TV salesman, or a politician. The widow takes care not to be too close to him. For (she knows) the brother-in-law is considering whether he should lay his hand on her arm, or slide his arm across her shoulder. He is considering whether he should grip her hard, in an unmistakable embrace, or simply squeeze her hand, brush his lips against her cheek. . . . The widow is distracted by how, though her backbone seems to have been broken and splintered, she is managing to walk upright, and to disguise the discomfort she feels.

The widow sees with a little thrill of horror that the front door has been left ajar. . . .

The beginning. Just the beginning. Out of my control.

She will make sure that the door is closed securely behind the brother-in-law. She will lock it.

In a jovial voice the brother-in-law says: "Well, Claudia! I'll call you later tonight. Maybe drop by tomorrow. Will you be home around four p.m.?"

Quickly she tells him *No*. She will not be home.

"What about later? Early evening?"

How aggressive the brother-in-law is! How uncomfortably close to her he is standing, breathing his warm whiskey breath into her face as if daring her to push him away.

"Goodbye! I'm sorry, I can't talk any longer right now. . . ."

The widow would close the door after her unwanted visitor but with a malicious little grin the brother-in-law turns to grip her shoulders and pull her to him and press his fleshy lips against her tight-pursed lips—so quickly she can't push him away.

"No! Stop."

"For Christ's sake, Claudia! Get hold of yourself. You aren't the first person ever to have lost a 'loved one.' "

The brother-in-law speaks sneeringly. The damp close-set eyes flash with rage.

The brother-in-law shuts the front door behind him, hard. He is very angry, the widow knows. She can't resist the impulse to wipe at her mouth with the edge of her hand, in loathing.

From a window the widow watches the brother-in-law drive away from the house, erratically it seems. As if he would like to press his foot down hard on the gas pedal of his vehicle but is restraining himself. She thinks—*But he will return. How can I keep him away!*

She is feeling shaky, nauseated. She has neglected to eat since early morning. The remainder of the day—late afternoon, early evening, night—stretches before her like a devastated landscape.

When she returns to the living room she discovers the empty whiskey glass set carelessly on a mahogany coffee table. The rim is smudged from the brother-in-law's mouth. Somehow, the amber liquid must have splashed over the side of the glass for there is a faint ring on the beautiful wood tabletop, an irremediable stain.

She is living alone since James's death.

It is maddening to be asked, as the brother-in-law has asked, Will you sell the house?

With subtle insinuation, Will you sell this large house?

Yet worse, Have you considered getting a dog?

Well-intentioned friends, relatives, neighbors. Colleagues from the private school in which she teaches. Often she is unable to answer. Her throat closes up, her face flushes with pinpoints of heat. She sees these good people glancing at one another, concerned for her. A little frisson passes among them like a darting flame, their concern for the widow that links them as in an exciting conspiracy.

She has a fit of coughing. A thorn in her throat, she's unable to swallow. A thorn in a cookie brought to her by one of the well-intentioned, she had not wanted to bite into, but had bitten into that she might prove how recovered from shock she is, how normal she is, how normally she is eating, unwisely she'd bitten into the cookie accursed as a fairy tale cookie for she has no choice, such cookies must be bitten into. And she begins to choke for she can neither swallow the thorn nor cough it up.

"Claudia? Are you all right? Would you like a glass of water?"—the cries come fast and furious like bees.

Quickly she shakes her head *No no—no thank you.* Of course she is all right.

It is the widow's task to assure others, these many others, eager-eyed, greedy to be good at her expense, of course she is *all right.*

Her husband was a well-liked person, indeed well-loved. There is an unexpected burden in being the widow of a well-loved man. Your obligation is to assuage the grief of others. Your obligation is to be kind, thoughtful, generous, sympathetic at all times when all you want is to run away from the kindly prying eyes and find a darkened place in which to sleep, sleep, sleep and never again wake.

Children are brought to the widow's somber house. Staring-eyed children for whom death is a novelty that threatens to turn boring after just a few minutes.

Adults for whom the death of their dear friend James will provide some sort of instruction or educational interlude for their children.

A brash child who says *My mommy says your husband die-ed.*

The widow sees looks of shock, disapproval in the adult faces. Embarrassment in *Mommy*'s face. The widow wants to hide her own face, that the brash child will not see how his crude words have made her cry.

The widow stammers an excuse. Retreats to the kitchen.

The widow will not hear her visitors murmuring in the other room for they have pitched their voices low, and she would rather draw a sharp-edged butcher knife across her forearm than overhear what they are saying.

Has the widow become an object of fear? An object of terror?

Has she become *ugly?*

Has she become *old?*

She thinks of witches. Women without men to protect them. Women whose husbands have died. Women whose property might be annexed by rapacious neighbors. Fortunately, the widow does not live in barbarous times.

This widow is protected by the law. The husband left a detailed and fully executed will leaving her his entire property, his estate.

When the widow returns to the other room her guests smile at her nervously, worriedly. They have prepared something to tell her and it is the widow's oldest friend who rises to embrace her speaking of how James had "seen the best in everyone"—"brought out the best selves of everyone"—and the widow stands very still in the embrace, her arms limp at her sides, arms that are not wings, arms that lack the muscular power of wings to unfold, to lift the widow out of this embrace and to fly, fly away for her obligation is to submit to the commiseration of others and not scream at them *Go away all of you! For God's sake go away and leave me alone.*

"James! Darling, come look."

She has begun to sight the great blue heron more frequently, at unpredictable hours of the day.

She believes that there is just one great blue heron at the lake. At least, she has never seen more than one at a time.

The large predator bird is fascinating to her. There is something very beautiful about it—there is something very ugly about it.

On her walks the widow has discovered the solitary heron hunting for fish in a creek that empties into the lake, that bounds the edge of her property—standing in the slow-moving water very still, poised to strike.

For long minutes the heron remains unmoving. You might think that it isn't a living creature but something heraldic wrought of pewter, an ancient likeness. Then as an unwitting fish swims into view the heron is galvanized into action instantaneously, stabbing its beak into the water, thrashing its wings to keep its balance, emerging in triumph with a squirming fish in its bill.

It is a shocking sight! It is thrilling.

No sooner does the widow catch a glimpse of the fish caught in the heron's bill than the fish has disappeared, in a single swallow into the predator's gullet. The rapacity of nature is stunning. Here is raw, primitive hunger. Here is pure instinct, that bypasses consciousness.

Sometimes, if the fish is too large to be swallowed by the heron in a single gulp, or if the heron has been distracted by something close by, the heron will fly away with the live fish gleaming and squirming in its bill.

There is a particular horror in this. The widow stares transfixed. It is not so difficult to imagine a gigantic heron swooping at her, seizing her in its bill and bearing her away to—where?

The heron invariably flies to the farther side of the lake, and disappears into the marshland there. Its flight seems awkward, ungainly like a pelican's flight—the enormous slate-gray wings like an umbrella opening, legs dangling down. Almost, if you don't understand what a killing machine the heron is, and how precise its movements, there is something comical about it.

Except this isn't so, of course. The heron is as much a master of the air as other, seemingly more compact and graceful birds.

The widow is appalled, yet riveted: that reptilian fixedness to the heron's eyes. Obviously, the heron's eye must be sharp as an eagle's eye, to discern the movement of prey in a dense and often shadowed element like water.

The long thin stick-like legs, that dangle below as the bird flies flapping the great wings. The long S-curved neck, the long lethal beak of the hue of old, stained ivory.

Difficult to get very close to the vigilant bird but the widow has seen that it has a white-feathered face. Dark gray plumes run from its eyes to the back of its head, like a mask. There is a curious rather rakish dark-feathered quill of several inches jutting out at the back of the heron's head—this feature (she will discover) is found only in the male. Its wide wings are slate-colored with a faint tincture of blue most clearly sighted from below, as the heron flies overhead.

Yet it is strange, the bird is called a *great blue heron*. Most of its feathers are gray or a dusty red-brown: thighs, neck, chest.

She has heard the heron's cry many times now:

a hoarse, harsh croak like a bark. Impossible not to imagine that there is something derisive and triumphant in this cry.

"James, listen! We'd been hearing the great blue heron for years without realizing what it was. . . ."

The harsh cry is a mockery of the musical cries and calls of the songbirds that cluster close about the house, drawn to bird feeders. (She and James had always maintained bird feeders. Among her dearest memories are of James biting his lower lip in concentration as he poured seed into the transparent plastic feeders on the deck at the rear of the house in even the bitterest cold of winter.)

In books on her husband's shelves the widow has researched the great blue heron—*Ardea herodias*. Indeed the heron is a primitive creature, descended from dinosaurs: a flying carnivore.

Its prey is fish, frogs, small rodents, eggs of other birds, nestlings and small birds. Eagles, the heron's natural predators, are not native to this part of the Northeast.

Considering its size the heron is surprisingly light—the heaviest herons weigh just eight pounds. Its wingspan is thirty-six inches to fifty-four inches and its height is forty-five to fifty-five inches. It is described as a *wading bird* and its habitat is general in North America, primarily in wetlands.

She and James had favored the familiar songbirds—cardinals, titmice, chickadees, house wrens and sparrows of many species—and had less interest in the waterfowl, which often made a commotion on the lake; now, she is less interested in the small, tamer birds and is drawn more to the lake and the wetlands surrounding it.

In the night, the blood-chilling cry of the screech owl wakes her, but also comforts her. She keeps her window open, even on cold nights, not wanting to be spared.

She has come to recall the heron attacking the mallards' nests as an actual incident, shared with her husband. Vague in its context it is vivid in details and has come to seem the last time she and James had walked together along the lake shore, hand in hand.

Now I want only to do good. I want to be good.

If I am good the terrible thing that has happened will be reversed.

The cemetery is just ten minutes from the house. Very easy to drive there. No matter the weather.

It is not the cemetery favored by her husband's family which is in the affluent community of Fair Hills fifteen miles away. It is not the cemetery the widow was expected to have chosen in which to bury her husband—that is, her husband's "remains." Instead this is an old Presbyterian cemetery in a nearby village, dating to the 1770s. It is small, it is not so very well tended. It is no longer exclusively for members of the church but has become a municipal cemetery. The earliest grave markers, close behind the dour stone church, are a uniform dull gray whose chiseled letters are worn smooth with time and have become indecipherable. The markers themselves are thin as playing cards, nearly, tilted at odd, jaunty angles in the mossy earth.

More recent grave stones are substantial, stolid. Death appears to be weightier now. Words, dates are decipherable. *Dearest Mother. Beloved Husband. Dearest Daughter 1 Week Old.*

Each day in the late afternoon the widow visits the husband's grave which is still the most recent, the *freshest* of graves in the cemetery.

The grave stone the widow purchased for the husband is made of beautiful smooth-faced granite of the hue of ice, with a roughened edge. Not very large for James would not have wished anything conspicuous or showy or unnecessarily expensive.

In the earth, in a surprisingly heavy urn, the (deceased) husband's ashes.

No grass has (yet) appeared in the grave soil though the widow has scattered grass seed there.

(Are birds eating the seeds? She thinks so!)

It is consoling to the widow that so little seems to change in the cemetery from day to day, week to week. The tall grasses are mowed haphazardly. Most other visitors come earlier than she does and are gone by late afternoon. If there is any activity in the church it is limited to mornings. Rarely does the widow encounter another mourner and so she has (naïvely) come to feel safe here in this quiet place where no one knows her. . . .

"Excuse me, lady. What the hell are you doing?"

Today there has appeared in this usually deserted place a woman with a truculent pug face. Like a cartoon character this scowling person even stands with her hands on her hips.

Claudia is astonished! Her face flushes with embarrassment.

In the cemetery at the gravesite of a stranger buried near her husband she has been discovered on her knees energetically trimming weeds.

"That's my husband's grave, ma'am."

The voice is rude and jarring and the staring eyes suggest no amusement at Claudia's expense, no merriment. There is a subtle, just-perceptible emphasis on *my*.

Guiltily Claudia stammers that she comes often to the cemetery and thought she might just "pull a few weeds" where she saw them. . . . It is not possible to explain to this unfriendly person that untidiness makes her nervous and that she has become obsessed with a compulsion to *do good, be good*.

It is her life as a widow, wayward and adrift and yet compulsive, fated. After James's abrupt death it was suggested to her by the headmistress of her school that she take a leave of absence from teaching and so she'd agreed while doubting that it was a good idea.

A five-month *leave of absence* it was. Seeming to the widow at the outset something like a death sentence.

She has busied herself bringing fresh flowers to James's grave, and clearing away old flowers. She has kept the grasses trimmed neatly by James's grave though (she knows) it is an empty ritual, a gesture of futility, observed by no one except herself.

There is not much to tend at James's neat, new grave. Out of a dread of doing nothing as well as a wish to do something the widow has begun clearing away debris and weeds from adjoining graves.

Why do you need to keep busy, Claudia? All our busyness comes to the same end.

She knows! The widow knows this.

All the more reason to *keep busy*.

In the neglected cemetery the widow has been feeling sorry for those individuals, strangers to her and James, who have been buried here and (seemingly) forgotten by their families. James's nearest neighbor is *Beloved Husband and Father Todd A. Abernathy 1966–2011* whose pebbled stone marker is surrounded by unsightly tall grasses, thistles and dandelions.

Scattered in the grass are broken clay pots,

desiccated geraniums and pansies. Even the artificial sunflowers are frayed and faded as mere trash.

Claudia has begun bringing small gardening tools and gloves to the cemetery. She has not consciously decided to *do good,* it seems to have happened without her volition.

The only sincere way of *doing good* is to be anonymous. She has thought.

But now she has been discovered. Her behavior, reflected in a stranger's scowling face, does not seem so *good* after all.

Quickly she rises to her feet, brushes at her knees. She is feeling unpleasantly warm inside her dark tasteful clothes.

She hears her voice faltering and unconvincing: "I'm sorry! I didn't mean to surprise or upset you. I just like—I guess—to use my hands. . . . I come to the cemetery so often. . . ."

"Well. That's real kind of you."

Just barely the woman relents. Though the woman doesn't seem to be speaking ironically or meanly it is clear that she doesn't think much of Claudia's charity, that has cast an unflattering reflection upon her as a slipshod caretaker of the *Abernathy* grave.

Unlike Claudia who is always well dressed— (she is too insecure to dress otherwise)—the scowling woman wears rumpled clothing, soiled jeans and flip-flops on her pudgy feet. Her streaked-blond hair looks uncombed, her face is doughy-pale. She too is a widow whose loss has made her resentful and resigned like one standing out in the rain without an umbrella.

Claudia hears herself say impulsively that her husband is buried here also.

"He just—it was back in April—died. . . ."

It is unlike the widow to speak so openly. In fact it is unlike the widow to speak of her personal life at all to a stranger.

Claudia has no idea what she is saying or why she feels compelled to speak to this stranger who is not encouraging her, whose expression has turned sour. Her brain is flooded as with a barrage of lights. *How have you continued to live as a widow? How did you forgive yourself? Why will you not smile at me? Why will you not even look at me?*

"O.K. But in the future maybe mind your own business, ma'am? Like the rest of us mind ours."

Rudely the woman turns her back on Claudia. Or maybe she has not meant to be rude, only just decisive.

Claudia returns to James's grave but she is very distracted, her hands are trembling. Why is the woman so hostile to her? Was it such a terrible thing, to have dared to pull out weeds on a neighboring grave?

Forget her. It's over. None of this matters—of course.

It is ironic, Claudia manages to elude friends, family, relatives who express concern for her, and worry that she is in a precarious mental state still; yet here in the cemetery, where Claudia would speak to another mourner, she has been rebuffed.

At James's gravesite she stands uncertain. She is grateful that in some way (her brain is dazzled, she is not thinking clearly) her deceased husband has been spared this embarrassing exchange. She is still wearing gardening gloves, and carrying her hand trowel. Her leather handbag is lying in the grass as if she'd flung it down carelessly. Why is she so upset, over a trifle? A stranger's rudeness? Or is she right to feel guilty, has she been intrusive and condescending? A quiet woman, one of the softer-spoken teachers at her school, Claudia has occasionally been criticized as aloof, indifferent to both students and colleagues. She winces to think how unfair this judgment is.

She doesn't want to leave the cemetery too soon for the woman will notice and sneer at her departing back. On the other hand, she doesn't want to linger in this place that feels inhospitable to her. She dreads someone else coming to join the scowling woman, and the scowling woman will tell her what she'd discovered Claudia doing at Todd Abernathy's grave, and what Claudia had done will be misinterpreted, misconstrued as a kind of vandalism.

High overhead is a solitary, circling bird. Claudia has been aware of this bird for some minutes but has not glanced up since she supposes it must be a hawk, hawks are common in this area, and not a great blue heron for there isn't a lake or wetlands nearby. . . .

She wants to think that it is a great blue heron. Her heart is stirred as a shadow with enormous outflung wings and trailing spindly legs glides past her on the ground and vanishes.

"Ma'am?"—the scowling woman is speaking to her.

"Yes?"

"There were potted geraniums on my husband's grave. Did you take them?"

"Potted geraniums? No . . ."

"Yes! There were potted geraniums here. What did you do with them?"

Hesitantly Claudia tells the woman that she might have seen some broken clay pots in the grass, but not geranium plants; that is, not living plants. She might have seen dead plants. . . .

"And some artificial flowers? In a pot here?"

"N-No . . . I don't think so."

"Ma'am, I think you are lying. I think you've been stealing things from graves. I'm going to report you. . . ."

Claudia protests she has not been stealing anything. She has cleared away debris and dried flowers, and pulled weeds. . . . Everything she has cleared away is in a trash hcap at the edge of the cemetery. . . . But the scowling woman is speaking harshly, angrily; she has worked herself up into a peevish temper, and seems about to start shouting. Claudia is quite frightened. She wonders if she has blundered into a place of madness.

Is that what comes next, after grief? Is there no hope?

Abjectly Claudia apologizes again. In a flash of inspiration—in which she sees the jeering face of her brother-in-law—she offers to pay for the "missing" geranium plants.

"Here. Please. I'm truly sorry for the misunderstanding."

Out of her wallet she removes several ten-dollar bills. Her hands are shaking. (She sees the woman greedily staring at her wallet, and at her dark leather bag.) The bills she hands to the woman who accepts them with a look of disdain as if she is doing Claudia a favor by taking a bribe, and not reporting her.

With sour satisfaction the woman says: "O.K., ma'am. Thanks. And like I say, next time mind your own damn business."

At her vehicle Claudia fumbles with the ignition key. She is conscious that her car is a handsome black BMW; the only other vehicle in the parking lot, a battered Chevrolet station wagon, must belong to the scowling woman. More evidence that Claudia is contemptible in some way, in the woman's derisive eyes.

She is very upset. She must escape. The cemetery, that has been a place of refuge for her, has become contaminated.

A shadow, or shadows, glides across the gleaming-black hood of the BMW. Her brain feels blinded as if a shutter had been thrown open to the sun. She feels a powerful urge to run back to the scowling woman bent over her husband's grave in a pretense of clearing away weeds. She would grip the woman's shoulders and shake, shake, shake—she would stab at the sour scowling face with something like a sharp beak. . . .

Of course the widow does nothing of the sort. In the gleaming-black BMW she drives back to the (empty) house on Aubergine Lake.

"Claudie? I'd like to drop by this afternoon, I have a proposal to make to you. . . ."

"No. I don't think so."

"I've been talking to a terrific agent at Sotheby's, you know they're only interested in exceptional properties. . . ."

"I said *No*. I won't be home, this isn't a good time."

"Tomorrow, then? Let's say four-thirty p.m.?"

"I—I won't be home then. I'll be at the cemetery."

"Fine! Great! I'll swing around to the house

and pick you up at about quarter to? How's that sound? I've been wanting to visit Jimmy's grave but have been crazy-busy for weeks and this is—the—ideal—opportunity for us to go together. *Thank you, Claudie.*"

Claudia tries to protest but the connection has been broken.

Your husband has left. Your husband has gone. Your husband will not be returning.

Calmly, cruelly the voice stalks her. Especially she is vulnerable when she is alone in the house.

Not her own voice but the voice of another speaking through her mouth numbed as with novocaine.

Your husband has left. Your husband has gone. . . .

Shaking out sleeping pills into the palm of her hand. Precious pills! One, two, three . . .

But the phone will ring if she tries to sleep. Even if there is no one to hear, the phone will ring. New messages will be left amid a succession of unanswered messages like eggs jammed into a nest and beginning to rot—*Claudia? Please call. We are concerned. We will come over if we don't hear from you. . . .*

The doorbell will ring. *He,* the rapacious brother-in-law, will be at the door.

"I will not. I've told you—*no.*"

Hastily she pulls on rubber boots, an old

L.L.Bean jacket of her husband's with a hood. She has found a pair of binoculars in one of James's closets and wears it around her neck tramping in the wetlands around the lake.

Here, the widow is not so vulnerable to the voice in her head. No telephone calls to harass her, no doorbell.

Rain is not a deterrent, she discovers. Waterfowl on the lake pay not the slightest heed even to pelting rain, it is their element and they thrive in it.

A sudden croaking cry, and she turns to see the great blue heron flying overhead. The enormous unfurled wings!—she stares after the bird in amazement.

Belatedly raising the binoculars to watch the heron fly across the lake. Slow pumping of the great wings, that bear the bird aloft with so little seeming effort.

Flying above the lake. Rain-rippled slate-colored lake. Chill gusty air, mists lifting from the water. Yet the heron's eyesight is so acute, the minute darting of a fish in the lake, glittery sheen of fish skin thirty feet below the heron in flight, is enough to alter the trajectory of the heron's flight in an instant as the heron abruptly changes course, plummets to the surface of the lake, seizes the (living, thrashing) fish in its bill—and continues its flight across the lake.

That stabbing beak! There has been nothing like this in the widow's life until now.

She is determined, she will be *a good person.*

James would want her to continue her life as she'd lived her life of more than fifty years essentially as *a good person.*

This catastrophe of her life, a deep wound invisible to others' eyes, she believes might be healed, or numbed. *If she is good.*

She forces herself to reply to emails. (So many! The line from *The Wasteland* seeps into her brain: *I had not thought that death had undone so many.*) She forces herself to reply to phone messages by (shrewdly, she thinks) calling friends, relatives, neighbors at times when she is reasonably sure no one will answer the phone.

Hi! It's Claudia. Sorry to have been so slow about returning your call   calls . . .

I'm really sorry! I hope you weren't worried . . .

You know, I think there is something wrong with my voice mail . . .

Of course—I am fine . . .

Of course—I am sleeping all right now . . .

Of course—it's a busy time for a—a widow . . .

Thanks for the invitation but—right now, I am a little preoccupied . . .

Thanks for the offer—you're very kind—but—

Yes I will hope to see you soon. Sometime soon . . .

No I just can't. I wish that I could . . .

Thank you but . . .

I'm so sorry. I've been selfish, I haven't thought of you.

The phone drops from her hand. She is trembling with rage.

Still the widow is determined to *do good, be good*.

She will establish a scholarship in her husband's name at the university from which he'd graduated with such distinction.

She will arrange for a memorial service for her husband, in some vague future time—"Before Thanksgiving, I think."

She will donate most of his clothes to worthy charities including those beautiful woolen sweaters she'd given him, those many neckties and those suits and sport coats she'd helped him select, how many shirts, how many shoes, how many socks she cannot bear to think, she cannot bear to remove the husband's beautiful clothing from closets, she will not even remove the husband's socks and underwear from drawers, she has changed her mind and will not donate most of his clothes, indeed any of his clothes to worthy charities. *She will not.*

That hoarse, harsh cry!—it has been ripped from her throat.

Flying, ascending. The misty air above the lake is revealed to be textured like fabric. It is not thin, invisible, of no discernible substance but rather this air is thick enough for the great pumping wings to fasten onto that she might climb, climb, climb with little effort.

She has become a winged being climbing the gusty air like steps. Elation fills her heart. She has never been so happy. Every pulse in her being rings, pounds, beats, shudders with joy. The tough muscle in her bony chest fast-beating like a metronome.

Low over the lake she flies. Through ascending columns of mist she flies. The great blue heron is the first of the predator birds to wake each morning in the chill twilight before dawn. It is an almost unbearable happiness, pumping the great gray-feathered wings that are so much larger than the slender body they might wrap the body inside them, and hide it.

Into the marshy woods, flying low. Her sharp eyes fixed on the ground. Small rodents are her prey. Small unwitting birds are her prey.

She will wade in the shallow water moving slowly forward on her spindly legs, or standing very still. She is very patient. Her beak strikes, she swallows her prey whole, and alive—thrashing and squealing in terror.

The hoarse, croaking cry—a proclamation of pure joy.

Yet she is happiest when flying. When she is rising with the air currents, soaring and floating on gusts of wind. When her eye detects motion below, a flash of color, fish color, and her slender body instantaneously becomes a sleek missile, aimed downward, propelled sharply downward, to kill.

Through the air she plunges and her sharp beak is precise and pitiless spearing a small fish which in a single reflex she swallows alive, still squirming as it passes down her throat, into her gullet.

She hunts without ceasing for she is always hungry. It is hunger that drives all motion, like waves that never come to an end but are renewed, refreshed.

Again the triumphant cry which you hear in your sleep. *I am alive, I am here, I am myself and I am hungry.*

Each morning it has been happening. The widow wakes with a sudden violence as if she has been yanked into consciousness.

A hoarse croaking cry from the lake.

A blinding light flooding the brain.

She is furious with the (deceased) husband. She has told no one.

Why did you go away when you did? Why did you not take better care of yourself? Why were you careless of both our lives?

How can I forgive you. . . .

Why had he died, why when he might not have died. As he'd lived quietly, unobtrusively. Always *a good person.*

Always *kind. Considerate of others.*

He'd had chest pains, a spell of breathlessness and light-headedness but he had not wanted to tell her. He'd promised he would pick up his sister's son at Newark Airport and drive him to relatives in Stamford, Connecticut; no reason the nineteen-year-old couldn't take a bus or a taxi but James had insisted, no trouble, really no trouble, in fact it is a good deal of trouble, it is a trip of hours, and some of these in heavy traffic. Already as he was preparing to leave she'd seen something in his face, a sudden small wince, a startled concentration, with wifely concern asking, Is something wrong? and quickly he'd said No, it's nothing, of course James would quickly say *It's nothing* for that is the kind of man James was. And that is why (the widow thinks bitterly) James is not that man any longer, he is not *is,* he is *was.* And she might have known this. She might have perceived this. Asking, But are you in pain?—and he'd denied pain as a wrongdoer would deny having done wrong for that is how he was.

She was saying, there was pettishness in her voice (she knows), Why don't we hire a car service for your nephew, explain that the drive is just too much for you, and then you have to turn around and return and we would pay for it ourselves of course, but James said Certainly not, no, he'd promised to pick up his nephew and drive him to Stamford, it would be an opportunity for him and Andy to talk together, for they so rarely saw each other in recent years. And he said my sister and brother-in-law wouldn't allow us to pay for a car service which seemed beside the point to Claudia who said exasperated, Then they should pay for the car! *Why are we quarreling, what is this about?*

Well, she knew. She knew what it was about: James's feelings of obligation to his family. James's habit of being *good*. His compulsion to *do the right thing* even when the *right thing* is meaningless.

Even when *the right thing* will cost him his life.

The husband's compulsion to be generous, to be kind, to be considerate of others because *that is his nature*.

And the pains had not subsided but increased as James drove along the turnpike and in a nightmare of interstate traffic his vehicle swerved off the highway just before the exit for Newark Airport. And he was taken by ambulance to an ER in Newark where he would survive for ninety-six minutes—until just before the terrified wife arrives.

Exhausted insomniac hours at her husband's death going through accounts, bank statements, paying bills.

Not death, *desk*. She'd meant.

The brother-in-law has left a glossy Sotheby's brochure.

The brother-in-law has left a glossy brochure for a "genetic modification" research institute in Hudson Park, New Jersey, across which he has scrawled *Terrific opportunities for investment here but it's "time sensitive"—before the stock takes off into the stratosphere.*

The brother-in-law has left a snide phone message—*Claudie? You must know that I am your friend & (you must know) you have not so many friends now that Jim is gone.*

She is not unhappy! She has grown to love rain-lashed days, days when there is no sun, mud days, when she can tramp in the wetlands in rubber boots. In an old L.L.Bean jacket of her husband's with wonderful zippered pockets and flaps into which she can shove tissues, gloves, even a cell phone.

She will not usually answer the cell phone if it rings. But she feels an obligation to see who might wish to speak with her. Whom she might call back.

Not the brother-in-law. Not *him*.

She is returning to the house when she sees his vehicle in the driveway—a brass-colored Land Rover. She knows that he is ringing the door-bell, rapping his knuckles smartly on the door.

She sees him peering through a window, shading his small bright eyes. *Claudie? Claudie it's me—are you in there?*

Amid dripping trees at the corner of the house the widow waits, in hiding.

She will say *It is very quiet at the lake. It is lonely at the lake.*

Most days.

"Stop! Stop that. . . ."

Cupping her hands to her mouth, shouting at the boys throwing rocks out onto the lake at the waterfowl.

It is amazing to the widow—she is *shouting*.

Not for years, not in memory has she *shouted*. The effort is stunning, her throat feels scraped as with a rough-edged blade.

"Stop! *Stop.* . . ."

Most of the rocks thrown by the boys fall short. Only a few of the youngest, most vulnerable birds have been struck—ducklings, goslings. The boys, who appear to be between the ages of ten and thirteen, are not wading in the water—(it's as if they are too lazy, too negligent to hunt their prey with much energy)—but run along the lake shore hooting and yelling. The adult mallards, geese, swans have escaped toward the center of the lake, flapping their wings in distress, squawking, shrieking. The boys laugh uproariously—the birds' terror is hilarious to them. Claudia is furious, disgusted.

"Stop! I'll call the police. . . ."

Boldly Claudia approaches the boys hoping to frighten them off. She is panting, her heart is pounding with adrenaline. She seems oblivious to the possibility that the boys might turn to throw rocks at *her.*

Their crude cruel faces are distorted with glee. They seem scarcely human to her. They glare at her, leer at her, trying to determine (she guesses) if she is someone who might recognize them and tell their parents; if she is someone whose authority they should respect.

"Don't you hear me? I said *stop!* It's against the law, 'cruelty to animals'—I will report you to the sheriff's office. . . ."

The words *sheriff's office* seems to make an impression on the older boys who begin to back off. Claudia hears them muttering *Go to hell lady, fuck you lady* amid derisive laughter but they have turned away and are tramping back through the marsh to the road.

Six boys in all. It is disconcerting to see how unrepentant they are, and how young.

Claudia supposes the boys live nearby. Not on the lake but near. Their laughter wafts across the marsh. She is shaken by their cruelty, and the stupidity of their cruelty. What would James have done!

On the lake the terrified birds continue their

protests, *craw-craw-craw*. They are swimming in frantic circles. They can't comprehend what has happened to their young, what devastation has rained down upon them. The widow is terribly upset and can't come closer to the carnage. A number of the young birds must have been killed in the barrage of rocks. Others must have been injured. She does not want to see the living, injured creatures floating in the lake. She does not want to see their writhing little wings, she does not want to see the distress of the elder birds, this has been enough, this has been more than enough, she does not want to feel anything further, not at this time.

And yet: pursuing the boys from the air. Beating her great wings, that are powerful with muscle. Glancing up they see her bearing upon them, their faces are rapt with astonishment, shock, terror. It would seem to them (perhaps) that the creatures they had tormented had taken a single, singular shape to pursue them. It would seem to them (perhaps) that a primitive justice is being enacted. The creature that swoops upon them is not a large predator, not an eagle. But her slate-colored outspread wings are as large as the wings of an eagle. Her beak is longer than the beak of an eagle, and it is sharper. The screams of the cruel boys will not deter her—nothing will deter her.

The boys run, stumble, fall to their knees

before reaching the road. They try to shield their faces with their uplifted arms. She is fierce in her assault, she attacks them with both her wings as an aroused swan would attack, beating them down, knocking them to the ground. And once they are on the ground they are helpless to escape the talon-claws that grip them tight as with her pitiless beak she stabs, stabs, stabs at heads, scalps, faces, eyes.

The boys' cries are piteous, pleading. Blood oozes from a dozen wounds and darkens the marsh grasses beneath them.

Her dreams have become agitated, she is afraid to sleep.

Especially, she is afraid to sleep in the large bedroom in the upstairs rear of the house over-looking the lake.

She moves to another, smaller room, a guest room overlooking the front lawn of the house. This room has pale-yellow chintz walls, organdy curtains. She keeps the windows shut at night. She is determined, she will regain her soul.

She will *make amends*.

"Why, Claudia! Hello."

"Claudia! What a surprise. . . ."

Greetings are warm at the private girls' school to which she returns for a visit. It has been too long, she says: four months, two weeks, six days! She has missed them all.

Unable not to see how, irresistibly, uncannily, every colleague she meets, everyone who shakes or grips her hand, embraces her, exclaims how much she has been missed, glances at the third finger of her left hand: the rings the widow (of course) continues to wear.

Do you expect to see nothing there? But of course I am still married.

In the seminar room she meets with her honors students.

These are bright lovely girls who have missed their favorite instructor very much. They all know that her husband has died and are shy in her presence. Several girls had written to her, halting little letters she'd read with tears in her eyes, and had set aside, meaning to answer some time in the future as she means to answer all of the letters she has received some time in the future.

The girls do not glance at the widow's rings, however. They are too young, they have no idea.

(But—what is wrong? Is something wrong? In the midst of an earnest discussion of that poem by Emily Dickinson that begins *After great pain, a formal feeling comes* the widow begins to feel faint, light-headed.)

Perhaps it is too soon for the widow to return to the school where she'd once been so happy, as she'd been younger. Too soon to be talking animatedly with bright young girl students as if she were as untouched as they, stretching her wound of a mouth into a smile.

Later, speaking with colleagues in the faculty lounge she feels an overwhelming urge to flee, to run away and hide. Her arms ache at the shoulders, badly she wants to spread the enormous muscled wings and fly, fly away where no one knows her.

She excuses herself, stumbling into a restroom. All her colleagues are women, their voices are pitched low in concern she wishes avidly not to hear—*Poor Claudia! She looks as if she hasn't been sleeping in weeks.*

Jangling at the front door. The widow would run away to hide but she cannot for she is powerless to keep the intruder out of her home.

Claudie he calls her in his mock-chiding voice laying his heavy hand on her arm as if he has the right.

Has she made a decision about the house?— the brother-in-law inquires with a frown.

Listing the property with Sotheby's as he has urged. Exceptional private homes, estates. The brother-in-law has contacted a realtor who can come to meet with them within the hour if he is summoned.

No she has told him. *No nono.*

And the pharmaceutical research company? It is "urgent" to invest before another day passes, the brother-in-law has tried to explain.

The brother-in-law is bemused by her—is he? Or is the brother-in-law exasperated, annoyed?

Badly he wants to be the executor of his deceased brother's estate for (of course) the grieving widow is not capable of being the executrix.

I will help you, Claudie. You know Jim would want you to trust me.

She sees how he is eyeing her, the small bright eyes running over her like ants. He is very close to her, looming over her about to seize her by the shoulders to press his wet fleshy mouth against her mouth but she is too quick for him, she has pushed away from him, breathless, excited.

Claudie! What the hell d'you think you are doing. . . .

He is flush-faced and panting. He would grab her, to hurt her. But she eludes him, her arms lengthening into wings, her slender body becoming even thinner, pure muscle. Her neck lengthens, curved like a snake.

And there is the beak: long, sharp, lethal.

The brother-in-law is dazed and confounded. In quicksilver ripples the change has come over her, it is the most exquisite sensation, indescribable.

She is above the enemy, plunging at him with her sharp long beak. So swiftly it has happened, the enemy has no way of protecting himself.

The great blue heron is swooping at him, he is terrified trying with his arms to shield his head, face, eyes as the beak stabs at him—left cheek, left eye, moaning mouth, throat—blood spurts onto the beautiful slate-gray feathers of the heron's breast as the enemy screams in terror and pain.

Afterward she will wonder whether some of the terror lay in the brother-in-law's recognition of *her*—his brother's widow Claudia.

The exhilaration of the hunt! The heron is pitiless, unerring.

Once your prey has fallen it will not rise to its feet again. It will not escape your furious stabbing beak, there is no haste in the kill.

Once, two, three . . . The widow shakes out sleeping pills into the palm of her hand.

Badly she wants to sleep! To sleep, and not to wake.

On the cream-colored woolen carpet of the guest room with chintz walls, organdy curtains, just visible inside the doorway is the faintest smear of something liquid and dark the widow has not (yet) noticed.

"My God. What terrible news. . . ."

Yet it is perplexing news. That the brother-in-law has been killed in so strange a way, stabbed to death with something like an ice pick, or

251

attacked by a large bird—his skull pierced, both his eyes lacerated, multiple stab wounds in his chest, torso.

The brother-in-law was discovered in his vehicle, slumped over in the passenger's seat, several miles from his home.

(But closer to his home than to the widow's home on Aubergine Lake.)

He'd been missing overnight. No one in his family knew where he'd gone. In the brass-colored Land Rover, at the side of a country road, the brother-in-law had died of blood loss from his many wounds.

It was clear that the brother-in-law had died elsewhere, not in the vehicle in which there was not much blood.

Hearing this astonishing news the widow is stunned. How is it possible, the brother-in-law is—*dead?* It doesn't seem believable that anyone she knows can have been murdered, the victim of a "vicious" attack.

A man with "no known enemies"—it is being said.

Local police are describing the attack as "personal"—"a kind of execution." Not likely a random or opportunistic attack for the victim's wallet was not missing, his expensive new-model vehicle had not been stolen.

There are no suspects so far. There seem to have been no witnesses on the country road.

The murder of the brother-in-law has followed soon after the assault on six local boys by what two survivors of the assault described as "a big bird like an eagle" that flew at them "out of the sky with a stabbing beak"—injuries to the boys' heads, faces, eyes, torsos that closely resemble the injuries of the brother-in-law.

Four boys killed in the savage attack, two boys surviving in "critical condition." They'd been attacked in a marshy area near Lake Aubergine where there are no eagles, no large hawks, no predator birds of any species capable of attacking human beings, or with any history of attacking human beings.

Yet the survivors insist they'd been attacked by a *big bird out of the sky with a stabbing beak.*

Like the brother-in-law, each of the boys was blinded in the attack.

Their eyes badly wounded, past repair. Stabbed many times.

Trembling, the widow hangs up the phone.

She has heard about the boys—the deaths, the terrible injuries. She has not wanted to think that something so awful could take place so close to her own home and when police officers have come to ask her if she'd seen or heard anything, if she knew any of the boys or their families she'd said only that they were not neighbors of hers and her husband's, they lived miles away and she knew nothing of them.

I'm afraid that I have seen nothing, and I have heard nothing. It's very quiet here at the lake.

More astonishing to her is the news of her brother-in-law—dying so soon after her husband James.

How devastated their family is! She is no longer the most recent widow among the relatives.

The phone will continue to ring but the widow will not hear it for she has stepped outside the house. Her lungs crave fresh air, it has become difficult to breathe inside the house.

Outside, the lawn has become overgrown. She has terminated the contract with the lawn service for she prefers tall grasses, thistles, wildflowers of all kinds—these are beautiful to her, thrilling.

A shadow gliding in the grasses at her feet.

She looks up, shading her eyes. She is prepared to see the great blue heron in its solitary flight but sees to her surprise that there are two herons flying side by side, their great slate-gray wings outstretched as they soar, the wing tips virtually touching.

From below she can see the faint tinge of azure in the gray feathers. Such beautiful birds, flying in tandem! She has never seen such a sight, she is sure.

Transfixed the widow watches the herons fly together across the lake and out of sight.

That cry! Hoarse, not-human, fading almost at once. But in an instant she has been awakened.

Cries of nocturnal birds on the lake. Loons, owls, geese. In the marshy woods, screech owls. Herons.

Sleepily she moves into her husband's arms. She is very content in his arms, she doesn't want to wake fully, nor does she want her husband to wake. Consciousness is too painful a razor's edge drawn against an eye—never are you prepared for what you might see.

WELCOME TO FRIENDLY SKIES!

Ladies and gentlemen WELCOME to our friendly skies!

WELCOME aboard our North American Airways Boeing 878 Classic Aircraft! This is North American Airways Flight 443 to Amchitka, Alaska—Birdwatchers and Environmental Activists Special!

Our 182-passenger Boeing Classic this morning is under the able command of Captain Hiram Slatt, discharged from service in the United States Air Force mission in Afghanistan after six heroic deployments and now returned, following a restorative sabbatical at the VA Neuropsychiatric Hospital in Wheeling, West Virginia, to his "first love"—civilian piloting for North American Airways.

Captain Slatt has informed us that, once we are cleared for *takeoff,* our flying time will be between approximately seventeen and twenty-two hours depending upon ever-shifting Pacific Ocean air currents and the ability of our seasoned Classic 878 to withstand gale-force winds of 90 knots roaring "like a vast army of demons" (in Captain Slatt's colorful terminology) over the Arctic Circle.

As you have perhaps noticed Flight 443 is a full—i.e., "overbooked"—flight. Actually most North American Airways flights *are* overbooked —it is Airways protocol to persist in assuming that a certain percentage of passengers will simply fail to show up at the gate having somehow expired, or disappeared, en route. For those of you who boarded with tickets for seats already taken—North American Airways apologizes for this unforeseeable development. We have dealt with the emergency situation by assigning seats in four lavatories as well as in the hold and in designated areas of the overhead bin.

Therefore our request to passengers in Economy Plus, Economy, and Economy Minus is that you force your carry-ons beneath the seat in front of you; and what cannot be crammed into that space, or in the overhead bin, if no one is occupying the overhead bin, you must grip securely on your lap for the duration of the flight.

Passengers in First Class may give their drink orders now.

SECURITY:

Our Classic 878 aircraft is fully "secured": that is, we have on board several (unidentified, incognito) Federal Marshals for the protection of our passengers. Under Federal Aviation Regulations, no Federal Marshal, pilot or co-pilot, or crew member is allowed a firearm on board any aircraft, for obvious reasons. However, under extenuating circumstances, in the event of the aircraft being forced to land unlawfully, a pilot of the rank of captain or above is allowed one "concealed weapon" (in Captain Slatt's case, a .45-caliber handgun worn on his person); with the captain's permission, his co-pilot is similarly allowed a concealed weapon. (In this case, co-pilot Lieutenant M. Crisco, much-decorated ex–Navy pilot, is also armed with a .45-caliber handgun.) Federal Marshals are armed with Tasers of the highest voltage, virtually as lethal as more conventional weapons, which, as they say, they "will not hesitate to use if provoked."

As passenger security comes first with us, all passengers are forewarned that it is not in their best interests to behave in any way that might be construed as "aggressive"—"threatening"—"subversive"—"suspicious" by security officers. All passengers are urged to report to the nearest flight attendant any suspicious behavior, verbal expressions, facial tics and mannerisms exhibited by fellow passengers; this includes the perusal of suspicious and "subversive" reading material. As Homeland Security advises us: "If you see something, say something."

To which Captain Slatt has amended grimly: "See it, slay it."

Note also: Federal Aviation Regulations require

passengers to comply with the lighted information signs and crew member instructions. Please observe the NO SMOKING sign which will remain illuminated through the duration of the flight; smoking is prohibited throughout the cabin and in the lavatories though allowed, under special circumstances, in the cockpit. All lavatories are equipped with smoke detection systems and Federal Law prohibits tampering with, disabling, or destroying these systems; accordingly, Federal Marshals are deputized to punish violators of this regulation at once, and harshly.

We will quote Captain Slatt in a more waggish mood: "If you smoke, you croak."

We crew members of North American Airways are here to ensure that you have a comfortable trip but we are primarily concerned about your SAFETY. With that in mind we ask that you take the North American Airways Safety Information Card out of the seat pocket in front of you and follow along as we perform our SAFETY demonstration.

SEAT BELT:

Our first and most important safety feature is the SEAT BELT.

Now that you are all comfortably seated please follow instructions: to fasten your seat belt, insert the metal fitting into the buckle until you hear a sharp *click!* If some of you are (as we noticed with derisive little chuckles as you'd shuffled on board) "plus-size" you may have some difficulty fitting your belt across your paunch; simply ring your overhead service bell and an airflight attendant, or two, or three as the case may be, will force the belt in place. The ensuing *click!* means that the belt is *securely locked in place.* Next, adjust your SEAT BELT to fit snugly with the loose end of the strap. Your SEAT BELT should be worn low and tight across your lap like a leather belt that has, for some obscure reason, slipped from your waist to bind you tightly across the thighs like a vise that will prevent your pants from "falling down" as well as pulling them taut to ensure a proper crease even in the event of aircraft catastrophe.

Yes, your SEAT BELT *is* locked in place. (Didn't I just tell you this? Why are some of you struggling to *unlock your locked* seat belts, if you have been listening?) Flight 443 to Amchitka, Alaska, is a very special flight. Article 19 of Homeland Security Provisions allows for specially regulated flights over "nondomestic" (i.e., foreign) territories to suspend "buckle release" privileges for such duration of time as the captain of the aircraft deems necessary for purposes of safety and passenger control.

Use of lavatories on this flight has been suspended, for reasons explained. So you can see there is no practical purpose in your seat belts not being *locked*.

In any case you have all signed waivers (perhaps under the impression that you were signing up for Frequent Flier credits) that grant to the flight captain a wide range of discriminatory powers for security purposes. (Such waivers are fully legal documents under Federal Statute 9584, Homeland Security.)

EMERGENCY EXITS:

Those passengers who unwittingly find themselves in "emergency exit rows" are expected to assist our (badly understaffed) flight attendant team in the (unlikely) event of an emergency. Namely, you will be expected to *struggle to open the very heavy exit door* which might be warped, stuck, or in some other way unopenable, even as terrified fellow passengers are pushing against you and trampling you amid the chaos of a crash or forced landing.

Passengers who believe that they are not capable of such courageous and selfless altruism in a time of emergency should raise their hands at once to have their seats reassigned.

("Reassigned" where?—that, you will discover.)

EMERGENCY MEASURES:

In the (unlikely) event of an EMERGENCY your seat belts are guaranteed to "pop open" to free you. And in the (unlikely) event that your seat belt is malfunctioning and remains in *lock* mode, a flight attendant will help you extricate yourself, if there are any flight attendants still remaining in the cabin after the emergency announcement.

As you are on a Boeing 878 Classic aircraft you will find that there are ten emergency exits of which the majority are in the First Class and Economy Plus compartments. A map of the aircraft will indicate five doors on the left and five doors on the right, each clearly marked with a red EXIT sign overhead.

All doors (except the overwing doors at 3 left and 3 right) are equipped with slide / rafts (except in those instances in which the overwing doors are at 5 left and 7 right). These rafts are intended to be detached in the event of a WATER EVACUATION. The overwing doors are equipped with a ramp and an off-wing slide. (A thirty-foot "slide" into icy waters is an astonishing visceral experience, survivors have claimed. Some have confirmed that the slide was a "life altering" experience not unlike the euphoria induced by an epileptic attack or a "near-death" experience and that they "believe they are more spiritual persons for having lived through it.")

Life rafts are located in "pull-down" ceiling compartments at the overwing doors. For our passengers in First Class, your escape routes near the front of the aircraft are clearly marked: FIRST CLASS EXIT. Passengers in Economy Plus, Economy, Economy Minus, Overhead Bin, and Hold are advised to locate the two exits nearest you, if you can find them; two exits is preferable to one, or none, in case one exit is blocked by crammed and crushed bodies or by flaming debris. Detailed instructions regarding slides and rafts are available in cartoon illustrations in the safety information card for slower-witted passengers or for passengers in states of extreme apprehension.

Though the odds of survival in the freezing waters of the Pacific Ocean even amid flaming wreckage are not high you will find in our air flight magazine *Friendly Skies Forever!* a monthly feature of interviews with passengers who somehow managed just this miraculous feat, in such hostile yet scenic environments as the Cape of Good Hope, the northern seacoast of Antarctica, the Bering Strait, and our destination today, the murky turbulent shark-infested icy waters of the Aleutian Islands strangely beloved by birdwatchers and environmentalists.

FLOOR-PATH LIGHTING:

This state-of-the-art aircraft is equipped with aisle-path lighting, which is located on the floor in the left and right aisles. In the event that "cabin visibility" is impaired—that is, in the event of a "blackout"—the exit path should be illuminated by these lights, except in those instances in which the "blackout" is total.

"White lights lead to red lights"—keep this favorite Zen koan of Captain Slatt in mind as the red light will indicate that you have reached or are near an emergency exit. If, that is, the red light is *on*.

OXYGEN:

Cabin pressure is controlled for your comfort. However, it may not be to everyone's comfort. North American Airways is mandated to maintain an air supply containing at least 18 percent oxygen (which may present difficulties for passengers with weak respiratory systems, asthma, extreme anxiety, or expectations of air with a minimum of 21 percent oxygen which is the "civilian norm"). Should the air pressure change radically in flight, which will happen at times, unpredictably, though at other times predictably, compartments are designed to automatically open in the panel above your head.

In the event of this emergency simply reach up—calmly!—and pull the mask to your face. Do not snatch at the mask desperately for masks made of flimsy materials have been known to "shred" in such situations.

Once the mask is on your face, oxygen should begin to flow. In the event that oxygen does not "flow" you may simply be, as Captain Slatt says, "out of luck"; or, if so minded, you may try to inveigle your seat mate into surrendering his or her mask, quickly before oxygen deprivation sets in and you begin to hallucinate.

Or, to raise the probability of your oxygen flowing unimpeded, you may purchase our OxFloLifeSave feature for just $400. (Airways staff will move among you to take orders now. Please raise your hands if you are interested in signing up for OxFloLifeSave rather than take your chances with "economy oxygen.")

Once you have firmly seized your mask place it carefully over your mouth and nose and secure with the elastic band as your flight attendant is demonstrating. Next, tighten by pulling on both ends of the elastic bands—not too hard, and not too hesitantly. In situations of chaos and terror "he who hesitates is lost"—but also, paradoxically, as Captain Slatt cautions, "he who acts impulsively is lost as well." Even though oxygen is flowing, at least in theory, the plastic bag may not inflate. This is estimated to occur in approximately 27 percent of aircraft emergency situations and it is just unfortunate! If you are traveling with children, or are seated next to someone who needs assistance, this is bad luck for them since you're obviously having enough trouble trying to secure your mask to your own face, and to breathe without hyperventilating; you certainly have no time for anyone else.

Warning: pure oxygen can be deleterious to the human brain, causing hallucinations, convulsions, blackouts, or stroke. Thus, while you should breathe deeply through your oxygen mask, *you should not breathe too deeply.*

Continue breathing through the mask until advised by a uniformed crew member to remove it. Do not—repeat: *do not*—surrender your oxygen mask to any individual who requests it if he or she is not in easily recognizable *North American Airways uniform.*

LIFE VEST:

Your life vest is located in a pouch beneath your seat. You may locate it now, to give yourself a "sense of security."

Should life vest use become necessary, remove your vest from the plastic packet as efficiently as possible, using both fingernails and incisors as required, but do not—repeat: *do not*—paw desperately at the packet which has been made toughly "child-proof" for the protection of our youngest passengers.

Once you have succeeded in tearing open the packet remove the life vest by using both hands, with a firm tug; slip the vest over your (lowered) head and pull smartly downward on the front panel with both hands exerting equal pressure. (Do not favor your strong hand over your weak hand as this may interfere with the operation of the life vest.) Next, bring the strap around your waist and insert it into the buckle on the front. (If there is no buckle on the front, you will have to fashion a "buckle" with the fingers and thumb of one hand—use your imagination!) Next, pull on the loose strap until the vest fits snugly—as I am now demonstrating. If you are a "plus-size" and your life vest does not fit— this is an unfortunate development you should have considered before you purchased your ticket to Amchitka, Alaska!

If you are a "minus-size" and it looks as if you are "drowning" in the life vest—this is very witty of you! You may well be quoted in *Friendly Skies Forever!* With your oxygen mask and your life vest you are now prepared to attempt to exit the aircraft amid a Dante-esque chaos of flames, boiling black smoke, dangling live electric wires, the screams and pleadings of your fellow passengers—or to, as Captain Slatt says, "walk the walk of Hell."

As you make your way out of the aircraft, by whatever desperate and improvised means, assuming you have located an exit that is unblocked, do not forget to INFLATE the vest by pulling down firmly on the red tabs. It is very important that you remember to INFLATE the life vest as an uninflated life vest is of no more worth in the choppy seas that await you than a soggy copy of *The New York Times* would be.

(In some rare cases, if the vest fails to INFLATE by way of the red tabs, it may be orally inflated by a strenuous, superhuman blowing into the inflation tubes at shoulder level, roughly equivalent, it has been estimated, to the effort required to blow up three hundred average-sized party balloons within a few minutes. Good luck with this!) For First Class passengers each vest is equipped with a "rescue light" on the shoulder for night use, which is water-activated by removing the Pull to Light tab located on the battery. In this way your life vest will provide for you a tiny, near-invisible "rescue light" in the choppy shark-infested waters of the night-time Pacific Ocean.

(It *is* complicated, isn't it! Each time we give our life vest demonstration something goes wrong, but it is never the same "something" from one time to another and so we have not the privilege of "learning from our mistakes"!)

"RETURN":

No Frequent Flier mileage is available for the "Return Flight 443"—there is no scheduled "Return Flight 443."

This "No Return" from Amchitka, Alaska, is stipulated in the waiver you cheerfully signed before boarding our aircraft without (it seems) having read, or perhaps even seen, the fine print.

APPLICATION:

Some of you are looking alarmed at the possibility of "No Return"—for reasons having to do with the Defense Department's Amchitka Bio-Labs Research Project which covers six hundred acres on the island though not marked on any (nonclassified) map, and which is your destination upon arrival at Amchitka.

Yes, this is a "surprise." Yes, it is too late to "exit."

Please note, however: less than 83 percent of passengers will be taken into custody as *subjects* in the bio-lab experiments; the remainder of you will be drafted as lab assistants and security staff, for there is considerable employee turn-over at Amchitka. Applications for these coveted positions should be filled out as soon as possible, as hiring decisions will be made before our arrival at Amchitka.

Please don't hesitate to raise your hand if you would like an application.

Note that the application requires a complete resume of education, background, employment, and financial assets. Now is not the time for "false modesty"!

PREPARATION FOR TAKEOFF:

Captain Slatt reports from the cockpit that the mysterious technical difficulties the aircraft has been exhibiting since your boarding ninety minutes ago have been deemed solved (at least by Homeland Security) and the aircraft is now ready for *takeoff*.

Accordingly, all doors have been locked; all SEAT BELTS are in *lock mode;* attendants, please be seated.

As some of you have discovered it is too late to change your mind about your exotic "bird-watching" expedition to the North Polar region. It was too late, in fact, as soon as you boarded the plane and took your seats. Therefore, please ensure that your seat backs and tray tables are in their full upright and stowed positions and all your carry-on items in secure places where they will not fly up suddenly and injure you or your hapless neighbors.

Ladies and gentlemen, we are now prepared to take off. We thank you for choosing North American Airways. Settle back in your seats, take a deep breath, and enjoy our friendly skies!

ACKNOWLEDGMENTS

"DIS MEM BER" originally appeared in *Boulevard* (2016).

"The Crawl Space" originally appeared in *Ellery Queen Mystery Magazine* (2016).

"Heartbreak" originally appeared in *Taking Aim*, edited by Michael Cart (HarperCollins, 2015).

"The Drowned Girl" originally appeared in *Boulevard* (2016).

"The Situations" originally appeared in *Vice* (2016).

"Great Blue Heron" originally appeared in *Black Feather: Bird Horror*, edited by Ellen Datlow (Pegasus, 2017).

"Welcome to Friendly Skies!" originally appeared in *Idaho Review* (2017).

Center Point Large Print
600 Brooks Road / PO Box 1
Thorndike, ME 04986-0001 USA

(207) 568-3717

US & Canada:
1 800 929-9108
www.centerpointlargeprint.com